Pr...
Nonfiction Book Pro...

D0568745

"The perfect tool with which to create a successful book proposal."
> —Mary Alice Kier and Anna Cottle, Cine/Lit Representation,
> Literary Agency and Media Consultants

"Elizabeth Lyon knows book proposals the way a surgeon knows anatomy."
> —Gary Provost, author of twenty-two books including
> *100 Ways to Improve Your Writing*

"This book is pure gold! I received an offer from a large publisher who stated that my proposal was professional and well-written; even my agent said it would be the standard in the industry. I owe a debt of gratitude to Ms. Lyon."
> —Mary Jeanne Menna, author of *Mom to New Mom:*
> *Practical Tips and Advice for the New Mom*

"Don't try to sell your next nonfiction book without consulting it."
> —Gerald Gross, author of *Editors on Editing:*
> *What Writers Need to Know About What Editors Do*

"*Nonfiction Book Proposals Anybody Can Write* gave me the structure I needed to produce a coherent, organized proposal. Everything my agent wanted to see in my proposal was there because of Elizabeth's book. I was able to send my proposal within a week, and three months later, my agent was responding to bids from four large publishing houses. One of them paid me an unusually high advance for a first-time author. I will always be grateful to Elizabeth."
> —Sallirae Henderson, M.Div., author of *A Life Complete:*
> *Emotional and Spiritual Growth for Midlife and Beyond*

A Writer's Guide to Nonfiction

ELIZABETH LYON

A Perigee Book

A Perigee Book
Published by The Berkley Publishing Group
A division of Penguin Putnam Inc.
375 Hudson Street
New York, New York 10014

Copyright © 2003 by Elizabeth Lyon
Text design by Tiffany Kukec
Cover design by Liz Sheehan

First edition: March 2003

Visit our website at www.penguinputnam.com

Library of Congress Cataloging-in-Publication Data

Lyon, Elizabeth, 1950–
   A writer's guide to nonfiction / Elizabeth Lyon.— 1st Perigee ed.
     p. cm. — (Writer's compass)
   Includes bibliographical references and index.
   ISBN 0-399-52867-9
   1. Authorship—Handbooks, manuals, etc.   2. Feature writing—Handbooks,
manuals, etc. I. Title. II. Series.

PN147 .L95   2003
808'.02—dc21
                                              2002035521

Printed in the United States of America

10 9 8 7 6 5 4 3 2

Dedicated to the memory of the writers
throughout the world
who lost their lives on September 11, 2001,
or during the aftermath,
and with that ending, lost the chance to share their dreams

CONTENTS

SOUTH:
Troubleshooting and Problem Solving

EAST:
Your Rising Star

WEST:
Refining Your Vision

ACKNOWLEDGMENTS

From conception to completion, this book, and the Writer's Compass series in particular, have received support and critique from my community of writers and editors. The freewheeling session at Oregon's Colonyhouse yielded the compass image with special thanks to brainstormers Martha Holmes, Patty Hyatt, Candy Davis, and Carol Craig.

The Writer's Retreat Workshop participants in 2000 and 2001, and the members of my three former critique groups, generously offered feedback on title ideas and, in some cases, on early drafts of the proposal. Thank you John Getze, Alice Wilson-Fried, and Roman White for your unflagging support, friendship, and critical opinion.

Privileged, humbled, and grateful fall short in describing the full extent of my feelings for four outstanding, independent book editors: Lorin Oberweger with Free Expressions; and Candy Davis, Carol Craig, and Ratina Wollner with Editing International. Sisters, I am in your debt. In addition, to the "cartel" members of Good Luck Marketing Club—Valerie Brooks, Patsy Hand, Skye Blaine, Mabel Armstrong, and Carol, Candy, and Ratina—you were my lifeboat during the roughest seas of this project.

Special thanks to my daughter, Elaine Carol Lyon, whose fresh imagination and artistic talent helped birth the design of the Compass series prototype. Special thanks as well to Lyndon Duke, whose visionary knowledge of the interactions of language, experience, and social change inform this work and my life.

As always, a cheering squad kept my spirits high when the going got tough. Thank you, cheerleaders all: Chicas Ricas, Bill Johnson, Jerry James, Carolyn Rose, Mike Nettleton, Kris Lyon, Louis Lyon, and my parents, Don and Ella Redditt.

Authors can only go so far with their ideas. Meredith Bernstein, my literary agent, and Jennifer Repo, my acquisitions editor, you both believed and invested in my vision, and I am grateful. Thank you, Christel Winkler, editorial assistant, for your support and enthusiasm. And, to Michelle Howry, you are this author's dream editor. You have understood my vision for this work and guided me toward making it fully realized.

INTRODUCTION

HAVE YOU EVER walked into a large bookstore and wondered, "Who buys all these books?" I have, and my answer is this: someone who hungers for knowledge and understanding. We each seek different books for diverse needs, whether for pleasure, necessity, power, relief of pain, or just curiosity. What feeds that hunger? The thirty thousand new nonfiction books published in the United States alone each year, and the thousands upon thousands of newspapers, magazines, and journals.

Have you also asked yourself why someone would want to read what *you* write? The answer: because you know something others don't know and need. You may not have thought about it before, but every person knows something, be it ever so small, that other people don't know. So far, each one of us is an original and that means no one else has had our exact experiences, not even our twin. At the very least, we each have a life story to share.

We reveal a great deal about ourselves by our reading habits. In my family, my father read *Popular Mechanics, Popular Science*, and tool catalogs. My mother read biographies and autobiographies and books on alternative health and metaphysics. I began reading what they read, although Dad's tool catalogs were far more esoteric to me than Mom's metaphysical literature. When my older brother and I as teens discovered the "marriage manual" hidden on the enclosed headboard shelf above my parents' bed, we pored over the contents. We *needed* the knowledge contained within that book.

What kinds of nonfiction did you grow up with? What do you read now and why? The scope of nonfiction subjects is as vast as the individuals who seek it, but what exactly is *nonfiction*? Is it merely "not fiction"? Some nonfiction writers have chafed at the absence of a more dignified term for their reality-based writing. In this time of "reality-based" TV, and of "creative nonfiction" and "autobiographical fiction," the lines are more blurred than ever. Indeed, the news often seems so edited and slanted as to be more fiction than fact. Even science has recognized the enormous impact of the observer on the observation, as well as the unavoidable filter of the researcher who interprets what was previously assumed to be "objective data."

Because fiction can also give readers a strong feeling of reality, what attracts some writers to nonfiction? I believe that many of us choose nonfiction because it is so compelling. It surpasses fiction by being "of the moment," full of the heartbeats of immediate or relevant experience. In that sense, nonfiction embodies a search for "absolute truth." Since we can never grasp reality, we have to keep trying to define it from different viewpoints.

For some of us, understanding our world through the subject area of our choice has the allure of being a child in a room full of toys. The invitation to explore is stronger than the invitation to create an imaginary counterpart.

Imagine a world without nonfiction. We would lose such potent life stories as *Man's Search for Meaning,* by Viktor Frankl; *The Autobiography of Malcolm X,* by Alex Haley and Malcolm X; *Anne Frank: The Diary of a Young Girl.* We'd never know *Into Thin Air,* by Jon Krakauer; *Angela's Ashes,* by Frank McCourt; or *Out of Africa,* by Isak Dinesen.

Gone would be biographies on Lincoln, Jefferson, Lindbergh, Einstein, Madame Curie, Florence Nightingale, Jane Goodall, or Oprah! We would lose all sense of history: *The Second World War,* by Winston Churchill; *The Making of the Atomic Bomb,* by Richard Rhodes; *Undaunted Courage: Meriweather Lewis, Thomas Jefferson, and the Opening of the American West,* by Stephen Ambrose.

Imagine the voices, all silenced, of social, political, humanitarian, and environmental reform. We would no longer have *Silent Spring,* by Rachel Carson; *Black Like Me,* by John Howard Griffin; or *Healing Our World,* by Mary Ruwart.

Bereft of the richness of the arts, ancient and modern, we'd lose our cultural heritage: *The Hero with a Thousand Faces,* by Joseph Campbell; *The Golden Bough,* by James George Frazer; *From Dawn to Decadence: 500 Years of Western Cultural Life,* by Jacques Barzun.

Vanished, all books of inquiry about our universe and our place in it: *The Double Helix,* by James D. Watson; *Principia Mathematica,* by Alfred North Whitehead and Bertrand Russell; *The Ants,* by Bert Hoelldobler and Edward O. Wilson; *The Birth of the Chaordic Age,* by Dee Hock. We'd have to ask, "Who is Stephen Hawking, Einstein, or Carl Sagan?"

Fast-forward to the last fifty years of self-help, everything from advice on child rearing (Dr. Spock to Dr. Laura), on spirituality (Norman Vincent Peale to Wayne Dyer), on religion (the Koran, the Bible) and on any and all aspects of daily life.

I have only scratched the surface of the body of nonfiction that forms the foundation of our lives. And now, we have the newest, unprecedented delivery system, the Internet, streamlining access to the collective body of information and news.

And here you are, wanting to add your voice—your ideas, inspiration, and knowledge—to that collective body. You want to write clearly and well, and yet the din of words may cause you to feel uncertain. How do you keep your footing? How do you know which way to go?

I decided to create a Writer's Compass series in the form of guidebooks. I wrote this book for writers of any kind, category, or length of nonfiction. The requirements I held for myself were clear organization, accessible instruction, and abundant examples. I also believe so fully in not divorcing the person from the writing that I wanted my books to address the heart and spirit of the writer.

To meet my reader's needs and the high standards I set for myself, I decided to organize this book by the four directions of the compass. It felt natural to assign North as the first section for getting one's bearings. As a result, North became the largest section of the book, showing how to map out nearly every kind of non-fiction a reader might choose.

As the president of a busy editing company, I know exactly how writers lose their way and, instead of ending up at a luxury hotel on the beach, they get stuck in quicksand. South, as in the vernacular "going south," became the part of the book to supply troubleshooting and problem-solving tools.

Over several decades, I've seen writers approach marketing with dread and trepidation, but it need not be so. East became the section where, built upon my prior two books, *Nonfiction Book Proposals Anybody Can Write* and *The Sell Your Novel Toolkit,* I could help readers over the hurdle of selling their writing.

Because writers are people, not just generators of words, I wanted to address more than issues of craft. As a result, West in the Writer's Compass series allows the reader to put his or her writing in perspective with more deeply held personal values and longings.

Remember, you're not entering a war zone to battle with your words; you're an explorer on an adventure of discovery. You have some ideas you want to share and express. You have a piece of yourself that you want to give to your readers, just like gifts brought back to family and friends by travelers throughout time. Your compass—this book—is in your backpack, so let's set out. I guarantee that I can help you make the journey worth it.

Elizabeth Lyon
Eugene, Oregon
www.elizabethlyon.com

NORTH

Getting Your
Bearings

ONE

What Do I Want to Say?

You have brains in your head.
You have feet in your shoes.
You can steer yourself any direction you choose.
                                        Dr. Seuss

WE WRITERS ARE explorers. The blank page is a wilderness awaiting discovery, a territory as uncharted as the geographic wild places of the world. We choose our level of difficulty. One person's hill may be another person's Kilimanjaro. The Great Smoky Mountains for you could be Mt. Everest for me. On some days, a simple essay or article might pose more challenge than an assault on a full-length memoir or biography.

Despite the individuality of our experience, as literary explorers we share similar needs. All of us need good maps and a compass to stay on course. Form and structure provide us with landmarks and trails. That's what this book and the Writer's Compass series supply.

Although many people describe writing as a solo journey, writers nearly always have an unseen, but vocal, companion who says, "Let's take that trail; I want to see the wildflowers." "Do you see that peak! I want to snap a picture." Who is this demanding companion? Let me introduce your reader. If you want to explore writing for its own sake, and you're uninterested in sharing your work, then you can afford to ignore the reader's needs. Most of us, however, want to share our writing. We want to get published. This book provides direction to those who want to share their writings with a wider audience, and that means paying attention to readers.

From the start, you can minimize confusion, irritation, or even abandonment by your intended readers simply by including them in your planning. Before you type a single word of a piece, stop and answer the following three questions:

- What is my **purpose** in writing this piece?

- What **promise** am I making to my readers?

- Does this piece **make a difference** in my readers' lives?

Purpose

The four main purposes of nonfiction are to:

- entertain
- inform
- inspire
- persuade

Dave Barry entertains. This book informs. Many essays inspire. Editorials persuade. Can a given piece of writing have more than one purpose? Definitely. However, one purpose should be primary. For instance, I could write a humorous essay about my one experience as a tour escort for a group of writers to a place I'd never been—the Yucatan, where I had to solve problems using broken pieces of a language I didn't speak—Spanish. While entertaining, this essay could have a persuasive message about American ethnocentrism and how Spanish should be as much a requirement in our school years as the three Rs. You can inspire while informing, entertain while persuading, or make any other combination, as long as you decide on one main purpose.

How does one decide upon a purpose? If you don't have a clear idea to begin with, quickly scribble a list of facets of your experience or angles about your subject. For instance, I recently had a chance to do this exercise in a workshop led by Elfrieda Abbe, editor in chief of *The Writer* magazine. For exercise purposes, I chose one of my favorite topics: Border collies. Within a few minutes, I'd generated the following list:

- Berlitz for dogs
- Teach your dog American Sign Language
- Increase your agility with dog agility training
- The three to five smartest breeds and how they're tested
- A history of smart dogs, from Rin Tin Tin and Lassie to the present
- Living with a Mensa dog, or "my Border collie is smarter than your honor student"
- Ten ways to increase your dog's IQ

For this exercise, I hadn't given any thought to purpose, and to tell the truth, I was just having fun. Even so, how does one select a purpose? After you create your list, which item compels you the most? Which one has "juice," meaning emotional charge? Once you know the answer to this question, you have your topic and from there, it's easy to figure out whether you want to inform, inspire, entertain, or persuade.

After I generated my list, I looked it over. Immediately, I knew that I was most drawn to "teach your dog American Sign Language." Why? I had seen a news feature about a woman who had saved deaf Dalmations who were going to be euthanized because they were deaf. She'd used sign language and said that her dogs knew about sixty words. Can you imagine? Besides being enthralled by this new idea, I was also moved by her mission to save these dogs.

The next step is deciding on a purpose. Again, which one draws you the most as applied to your idea? A teacher to the end, I knew that my primary purpose, if I wrote the article on using American sign with dogs, would be to inform. If you are still uncertain about how to select a purpose, you may gain clarity after reading the next sections on "promise" and "making a difference."

Promise

Once you've decided your purpose in writing, it becomes your promise to your reader as well as to yourself. For instance, all how-to writing promises its readers success when they follow step-by-step instructions. If you buy a book about how to construct a birdhouse, the promise is that you'll have a finished product when you've followed the instructions. But how often do we experience the promise of "some assembly required" only to discover, eight hours later and six parts leftover, that the step-by-step instructions were a joke?

Self-help, a particular kind of how-to writing, focuses on people rather than things. The reader is attracted to an article or book because it *promises* a solution to a specific problem. Self-help readers will latch onto your promise to relieve the condition for which they suffer: debt, loneliness, extra pounds, recalcitrant children, or too much clutter.

"Promise" takes on particular meaning when applied to writing about personal experiences. When you write about your life or about another person's life, your promise must extend beyond the purpose "to inform." The "story promise," as it is sometimes described, refers to a promise the writer makes to a reader to fulfill a universal human need. What are some of these universal needs? To belong, to love, to forgive, to survive. In the writing, this need or yearning is expressed or implied by the narrator and defines the emotional level of the story.

The universality of human suffering and triumph compels your reader—a stranger—to invest in your story. Most readers identify with the anguish of a parent whose child has leukemia and awaits a bone-marrow donor, even if they themselves have not experienced such a trauma. Such an essay, superficially about a child with a disease, is *really* about faith, a belief that many more readers can relate to. Faith is a universal issue of human experience and, in difficult times, something we yearn for.

The same story, however, could be written with a different story promise. After all, other people can experience the same, or similar, events, yet be affected in entirely different ways. Maybe another writer would take the same story and focus on her need for forgiveness, or for understanding, or for family unity. Faith, forgiveness, understanding, and family unity are promises for stories whose purposes could be to entertain, inform, inspire, or persuade.

Making a Difference

Most of us want to make a difference in our writing and in our lives. I first learned of this concept as applied to writing from Lyndon Duke, a visionary social scientist. Several decades ago, Duke postulated that one could categorize eras of human experience in terms of the fundamental question that "defined" the age . . . and the answer to that all-important question. Thus, the Middle Ages, he suggests, were defined by the question "Why?" The answer was "God's will." Our most recent era began about four hundred years ago when the early scientists' curiosity drove them to ask a different question: "How?" Science and technology have supplied the answer to this question, which has, according to Duke, defined our most recent era.

As predicted by Duke over a decade ago, we have recently entered a new era defined by a new question: "What difference can be made?" The question falls awkwardly on our ears, perhaps because we want to add the former era's word—how. *How* can I make a difference? Yet this question is not the same as the new question. "How" provides problem solving. "What difference can be made?" asks us to provide meaning.

Making-a-difference language is everywhere in our culture. "We make a difference" is the new slogan of commerce and, as shown by the nearly *three hundred* Amazon-listed books with that slogan in their titles, of literature. Duke said that the proliferation of the new question is the first step of a new era. The second step is quantifying and qualifying the difference that can be made. What specifically is that change? If there is no change—no difference made—then an action has had no meaning.

As a friend and mentor, Lyndon Duke urged me to start practicing defining exactly what difference I seek prior to beginning each piece of my writing. The trick is to avoid defining a difference you wish to accomplish in terms of what *you'd* like to get, such as money or recognition. Instead, this new way of thinking asks you to define what you wish *your reader* to receive. After all, if you intend to share your writing with an audience, you want them to be changed. This approach to your writing runs deeper than figuring out a purpose or even a promise; it taps the wellspring of our most important reasons for writing.

How many articles, essays, or books have you read and forgotten the instant you finished reading them? If, at the end of reading your writing, your reader has not been changed, then you have made no difference whatsoever. A waste!

The best way to use your writing to make a difference is to define what meaning you would like readers to carry with them. For instance, I have two sacred values in my life—personal power and individual freedom. I've always been a seeker, and my childhood was blessed with a mother who insisted that whatever I could imagine, I could do. Yet, the inner explorations that defined my teen and young-adult years led me to dwell on my limitations.

In 1988, an unexpected recommendation from a friend led me to shift careers and become a college writing instructor. His faith helped me focus on my potential instead of my limitations. Soon after I began teaching, I started my business as a book editor. Writing has always been a vehicle of empowerment and therefore of freedom. Helping writers gain mastery over the knowledge that will make them powerful has been my mission ever since. The specific difference I wish to make with all of my writing is to empower my readers.

And remember, not all writing need have lofty goals. When writing personal experiences or biographies, your own purpose and promise will lead you to consider how you hope your reader will be changed. Suppose you plan to write an essay, for instance, about

**SOME MAKE-A-DIFFERENCE
TITLES ON AMAZON.COM**

The Tipping Point: How Little Things Can Make a Big Difference
by Malcolm Gladwell

Boards That Make a Difference: A New Design for Leadership
by John Carver

Sisters in Strength: American Women Who Made a Difference
by Yona Zeldis McDonough

Kids Who Make a Difference by Gary Chandler and Kevin Graham

The Big Help Book: 365 Ways You Can Make a Difference by Volunteering
by Alan Goodman

Parents Do Make a Difference by Michele Borba

One Person Can Make a Difference by John Haase and H. C. Wolford

You Can Make a Difference by Jack Graham

*The Courage to Give: Inspiring Stories of People Who Triumphed over
Tragedy to Make a Difference in the World* by Jackie Walman, et. al.

52 Ways to Make a Difference by Lynn Gordon

You Make the Difference by Stan Hustad

Make a Difference by Bob Walling

Little Things Make a Big Difference by Laurin Sydney

The Difference Women Make by Michele L. Swers

how you stumbled across some antiques in London—antiques that
you recognized as priceless items stolen from the Crown several
centuries earlier. Suppose no one believes you; after all, how pre-
posterous! Your purpose in writing the story might be to entertain.
But at a deeper level, your humorous essay might promise an exploration of trust—in self or others, or perhaps of respect. Your
reader will be led to experience that promise—of trust or respect—

vicariously and come to a new understanding of it. To the extent that you succeed, your writing has made a difference.

All this talk of "making a difference" may seem unnecessarily philosophical if you plan to write an article about how to, say, improve your house's energy efficiency. However, if you combine your purpose in writing—to entertain, inform, inspire, or persuade—with a way you want to make a difference in your readers' lives, your writing will increase in its effectiveness. You'll be able to plumb the depths of your subject rather than render a superficial treatment.

Do we always need to write with such deliberation? Sometimes writers, myself included, write "from the hip," without any but the vaguest of plans for what goes on the paper. Unplanned or spontaneous writing has its place. We should take time to write whatever comes to mind without imposing a plan or structure. This kind of "free writing" belongs in every writer's repertoire. However, this book makes the case for mastering form and structure as a prerequisite for greater freedom and creativity later on. You may have heard the Zen expression "First there is a mountain, then there is no mountain, then there is." Applied to writing, first you become overly aware of form and structure, then it vanishes as a concern, and then it returns in your awareness without being oppressive. Eventually, it becomes an ally, not an enemy.

Beginning to think of your writing in terms of personal values, for instance, may be foreign to how you've previously thought about writing nonfiction. I'm going to ask you to write from the inside out, from your personal values. Expect to apply copious amounts of oil to those thinking joints.

The examples in Map 1-1 at the end of the chapter may help you combine the first of many new ideas about how to begin writing effective nonfiction.

RECOMMENDED READING

A Story Is a Promise by Bill Johnson

Writing a Book That Makes a Difference by Philip Gerard

The Right to Write by Julia Cameron

Theme

The idea of a theme for your writing may have mystified you when your English teacher first brought it up. "What is the theme of Dickens's *Great Expectations*?" is sure to have produced pin-drop silence.

But once you have figured out your story promise and you've arrived at a pretty good idea of the difference you hope your piece of writing will make with your reader, you're three-quarters of the way to knowing your theme.

"Theme" is the message carried away by the reader. If you look at the words listed under "promise" in Map 1-1, you'll see some examples of one-word themes: belonging, self-reliance, responsibility.

Why bother with a theme before you begin to write? For the same reason that explorers make detailed plans before leaving on a trek—this planning work will make the actual writing far easier. A piece with a theme translates into clarity for your reader. They sense your competence and relax.

Let's say that you plan to write a straightforward technical paper on new software for accountants. To theme or not to theme; that is the question. If you don't, the reader who wants to know the information will still value your writing. On the other hand, if you emphasize that with this new software, the accountant can save time and increase revenues, you add greater competency, efficiency, freedom, and probably many other benefits. If you reverse your emphasis from saving time and increasing revenues to greater competence, you're identifying a take-away message, a theme. "This article on cutting-edge software offers the busy accountant, CPA, or small-business owner increased competency in both simple and sophisticated aspects of accounting."

In essays, memoirs, and biographies, theme becomes the spine of the story. It is essential, not optional. Once you're able to define your theme, you can organize and write your piece with ease. After reading *Into Thin Air,* by Jon Krakauer, about an Everest climb that turned disastrous when a blizzard struck, the message that lingers for me is how selfishness costs lives. In contrast, *Facing the*

Extreme, a lesser-known memoir by Ruth Anne Kocour, describes her team's assault on Denali during a freak blizzard where many of the climbers died. The message that lingers after reading her book is increasing self-understanding. These two memoirs cover similar events but use dissimilar themes. Without a theme, a memoir is a mere recounting of events.

Subjects

For many writers, the subject they want to write about comes first and the meaning of it—for themselves and their readers—comes later. Consider these four subjects:

- Ideas
- Experiences
- Inanimate objects
- Living organisms

IDEAS

What are you preoccupied with? Mortality? Love? An answer to "Who am I?" and "What is the meaning of existence?" Perhaps your thoughts are of a more whimsical nature, and you wonder if sleeping in different-colored rooms will change your dreams.

Whether you want to explore the great philosophical questions of life or the small ideas that make each of us wonder, you'll never run out of ideas. Get in a rut and you can always turn to one of the many books that offer to help writers find ideas and develop their creativity. The resource box on page 13 lists seven.

Several of my writing friends have created their own "prompt" boxes (a bag, box, or empty container of any kind will work). They cut words and phrases from newspapers and magazines and drop them into their idea boxes. When they're "stuck" with their writing, they'll reach into their prompt box for inspiration. These prompts make ideal warm-up exercises. Some will capture enough interest that you'll want to develop them into an article, essay, or even a book.

EXPERIENCES

You've likely heard the writing maxim "Write what you know." When I first started to write, I didn't feel as if I knew enough to write about anything. In reality, each day of our lives churns out twenty-four hours worth of potential material. All of us are experts on our own lives, at least.

Research can supplement any area that holds your interest, whether you want to write about your hobby of collecting colored glass bottles or about your work as a substitute teacher. What every writer has at her fingertips are life's experiences. From the first time you dyed your hair to the last time you helped someone in need, you are teeming with experiences that could be written about. One of the mistakes that writers frequently make is trying to write about the big events of life or about an entire era. They get lost, or lose the reader, by trying to cover too much ground. Most of the time, they fail to create sufficient depth or meaning about what is important. Often, the most effective essays deal with a small experience where the writer can bring out a singular and powerful statement.

I remember an essay written by Carolyn Scott Kortge, a journalist and author who attended one of my critique groups. She wrote about the failure of a gas-station attendant to greet her or say the customary "Thank you—come again." By focusing on a gesture so small, she achieved far greater impact than if she had tried to write about the deterioration of common courtesies.

A good place to begin is by listing the experiences in your life that will fit the scope of writing you want to undertake. If you

RECOMMENDED READING

A Writer's Book of Days by Judy Reeves

Idea Catcher by the editors of Story Press

101 Writing Exercises by Lois J. Peterson

Writing Down the Bones by Natalie Goldberg

Writing in Flow by Susan Perry

How to Think Like Leonardo da Vinci by Michael J. Gelb

The Writer's Idea Book by Jack Heffron

FINDING WRITING IDEAS FROM LIFE

Birth	Vacations	Successes
Death	Work	Sudden Insights
School	Firsts	Enemies
Friends	Mentors	Relatives
Parents	Holidays	Crossroads
Dating	Coming of Age	Decisions
Sex	Accidents	World Events
Marriage	Illnesses	Natural Disasters
Divorce	Hard Times	Significant Dates
Fun	Mistakes	Wars
Children	Hobbies	Spiritual Experiences
Childhood	Travel	Milestones

wish, begin your list with the experiences most of us have had: births, deaths, marriages, divorces, illnesses, diseases, schools, jobs, vacations, pets, children, relatives, friends, and so forth. After you have written down as many of these categories (and you can personalize them) as spring to mind, mark which ones presently interest you.

Next, select one category and then make a new list that breaks your memory into smaller and smaller ones. For instance, let's say the category that draws you is mistakes. Which ones? Make a new list, or draw a cluster diagram where each spoke to the wheel of mistakes represents one of your boo-boos. Remember that time when you wore two different shoes to the Graduate Record Exam? How about the time when you looked down in the middle of class and saw that you were wearing two necklaces at a time when this was hardly vogue? Okay, those are two of my precious high-school memories when I goofed. Was I a nerdette? Don't ask. Each memory is a veritable gold mine for writing ideas. Explore!

INANIMATE OBJECTS

If your fascination runs toward "things," your subjects will be endless, and you'll never run out of places to sell your articles or books.

We Americans are obsessed not only with possessions but with inventions, toys, and tools of all kinds.

I am more of an experience and idea person than an inanimate object person, yet I recently felt compelled to write a column about ergonomic chairs and keyboards. I have friends who love to cook and can tell you about the best kitchen gadgets. Another friend of mine collects jawbreakers. Seriously! He can talk for half an hour about the different types, the history, designs, coatings, and contents. If the things of the world craze you, write about them! You can make a living doing so.

LIVING ORGANISMS

You'll find more demand for writing that is about people than iguanas, but if iguanas turn you on, you can find ways to share "everything you ever wanted to know about iguanas" with the rest of us. Even I have an iguana story. While visiting Costa Rica with my son's class, I became a "homestay sister" to a twelve-year-old girl. When I asked her about iguanas, she rolled her eyes and smacked her lips. "Mmmm," she said, *"iguana con huevos."* Iguana and eggs. Over easy or scrambled? Sans scales, I hope.

I've always found the creatures of the deep to be creepy, but when one of my students began reading her articles about the underwater world in my critique group, she changed all that. She made a difference by transferring her passion for the botany and biology that she had witnessed and photographed as a scuba diver. I'll never forget one piece she brought in titled "Sex and the Seahorse." Fascinating!

You may agree that taken literally, there really is nothing new under the sun. For a writer, you can always find a new angle. I've been amazed and absorbed, for instance, by the literature on essential oils from flowers and plants used for health and well-being. Twenty years ago, I doubt you would have been able to find anything written about this, but today, aromatherapy based on plant oils has found a place in nearly every big magazine.

Our most compelling living organism is Homo sapiens. Writing about people takes many forms. You can write profiles, features, personal experiences, biographies, and memoirs. People at work. People at play. Celebrities or your next-door neighbor. You can write about overcoming obstacles, building a career, or self-discovery. Make lists of topics and the people who interest you and add to it.

Once you decide what you want to say, you're on your way, and that unseen companion by your side is your ally, confidant, and map reader. But who are your readers, the people taking this journey with you?

MAP 1-1

Subject + Purpose + Promise = Making a Difference

Subject of Writing	Purpose	Promise	Making a Difference
finding a parking spot	to entertain	belonging	show commonality
the stay-at-home dad		tolerance	consciousness raising
the common cold worldwide		commonality	global peace
all about seahorses	to inform	wonder	appreciation of nature
improving marriage		family unity	end children's suffering
how to use Quicken		self-reliance	financial independence
egg-carton playhouses	to inspire	preservation	environmental values
Somalia's Good Shepherd		faith	build faith
fruit trees in parks		survival	eliminate hunger
secrets of lobbyists	to persuade	responsibility	citizen participation
advances in sun power		progress	stop dependency on gas
American isn't English		inclusiveness	bilingual education

TWO

Who Are My Readers?

I never travel without my diary.
One should always have something
sensational to read on the train.
                          Oscar Wilde

PROFESSOR MENTAL-GIANT-ALREADY THINKS he's writing *The Home Scientific Companion* for the general public, but he uses too many eight-syllable words and quasar examples. Motivational speaker Valerie Valiant thinks her book, *If I Can Do It You Can Do It*, is ideal for psychiatrists and psychologists, even though it is a book of platitudes. Too highbrow, too lowbrow; if you don't identify your reader, you're going to miss the mark.

Most writers spend little time determining the profile of their readers. While it involves guesswork, an educated guess is better than no guess at all. The following guidelines will help you define your audience:

- Know thyself
- Know thy demographics
- Know thy publications

Know Thyself

This command, a legacy from the Oracle of Delphi, offers the self as the first stop on the way to understanding anyone. Consider yourself the first reader of your work. For instance, the more educated a person is, the larger his vocabulary and the more likely he is to use multisyllabic and words with Latin origins. If you use lots of "big" words with "tion" and "sion" endings (Latinate), what reader would match your background? In all likelihood, your reader would be college educated, and he or she might hold a graduate degree. In this example, the reader is a mirror of the writer.

Every year I work editorially with professionals with master's degrees or doctorates who believe they are writing for the general public. Yet, their use of language includes multisyllabic words, high diction, and an excess of to-be verbs (is, was, were, be, being, been). I've coined a phrase to describe their problem: "higher-educationally impaired." Because they are blind to the correspondence between writing and readership, they have no idea that their work is unsalable to anyone but other scholars.

I've also had clients who wrote "hip" for a "straight" audience, and clients who used slang and idiosyncratic humor for "serious" magazines. Without being conscious of it, these writers were writing for just one reader—themselves.

Besides education, what is your background related to the subjects you've chosen to write about? If you work in a technical field, for instance, you'll have mastery over a particular kind of language that will be little known by the public. Be careful not to assume that your reader will know that "caries" are "cavities" if you're a dental technician, or that "GSR" is "galvanic skin response" if you're a biofeedback technician. Some readers may even need a definition of "biofeedback."

Have you set your sights on a national, or even international, readership? Despite the forces of consumerism and conformity, America—and other countries—still have regionalisms. A friend who lived in an Oregon fishing town once explained the difference between a "trawler" and a "troller." The first is a boat that drags a fishing net or bag, and the second (not a word in my dictionary) pulls bait behind it. When I moved to the Northwest, I noticed the common vocabulary of forestry. It seems as if the mills are always seeking choker-setters, green-chain pullers, and planers. Will all of your readers understand the terms you take for granted?

Another area of self-awareness involves beliefs, biases, and what I think of as conditioning. For instance, spirituality, as distinct from religion, is popular across all subject areas in nonfiction. Books such as Carolyn Myss's *Sacred Contracts* and Wayne Dyer's *There's a Spiritual Solution to Every Problem* are part of this spirituality genre. Yet, when I see words like "the Universe," "manifestation," and "abundance," I suspect the writer holds New Age beliefs as surely as the words "Christ," "sin," and "evil" suggest Christian beliefs. If either of these writers intends to "preach to the choir," then their vocabulary is fine. But if they intend to write for the general public, their beliefs, as reflected in their word choices, will alienate part of their readership.

A "bias" is an inclination or leaning. A "prejudice" is a preconceived idea or judgment, usually unfavorable. We all harbor biases and prejudices, and our writing will reflect them—whether we know it or not. Many writers mistakenly assume that their readers hold the same biases as they do. One thing is certain—your readers, or the publication that prints your ideas, will let you know if you offend them. You may remember the outcry from Muslims worldwide when President Bush used the word "crusade" shortly after September 11. To avoid public embarrassment, think about your biases and prejudices relative to your writing and reread your writing for anything that might offend. However, if you intend to offend, to raise some of your readers' ire, do so consciously and carefully, and be prepared to handle the consequences.

Despite the backlash against the concept of "politically correct," writers are expected to be gender sensitive (and race, religion, and ethnicity sensitive). I welcome it. Male pronouns and other male nouns, used to mean both genders, went unquestioned for hundreds of years. Not only do women comprise about half the population, they buy most of the books. When you think about yourself and your writing, consider whether you use male pronouns exclusively or words like *mankind*, *postman*, or *webmaster*. This level of awareness is a good start toward gender equity.

Know Thy Demographics

Demographics, the statistical study of populations, gives researchers information they need for all kinds of purposes. Like demographers, writers should think about their readers' gender, occupation, income, likes, dislikes, hobbies, social class, race, religion, marital status, and other sociological groupings. You won't need all of this data for every piece of writing—and you don't need to quantify it with statistics—but everything you can know about your reader will inform your writing.

I once consulted with an author who wanted to write a book for women on how to become financially secure. Her working title made reference to "the next million dollars." My question to her: "And who are your readers? Millionaires?" She hadn't considered whom she was writing for.

If you intend to write for magazines, you're in luck. Because advertisers want to match their products with the right consumer, magazines conduct studies that define their readers to supply potential advertisers with demographics, including statistics. You can request this information from the advertising department.

Writers of books must develop a whole section in their book proposals about their readers. Book proposals contain a marketing section in which authors must define and describe the primary readership, and often the secondary readership, of their proposed books. They must also describe the size of their market and use statistics if they are available. You may have written the best book available on ant farming, but editors want to be sure there's a market out there who's interested in buying it. It's your job to prove this.

You may think that breaking down the demographics of your potential reader is unnecessary if you are writing autobiography, either personal essays or a memoir. After all, you're writing about *your* life, and therefore your writing will reflect you, not the reader. Think again. It's just as important to know who is going to read your autobiographical work as it is for any other kind of nonfiction. Don't make the mistake of thinking that "everyone" will want to read your story—however unusual, shocking, or fascinating your life has been. There's a common cliché in publishing: "A book written for everyone is a book written for no one." Be realistic and define your audience.

Know Thy Publications

About forty to fifty thousand books are published each year in the United States, and literally thousands of magazines exist. Add in newsletters and Internet e-zines, and we're looking at a huge number of places for writers to sell their work.

What do you like to read? Are you going to write for these publications or for different ones? If you plan to write and publish a book, have you read books on your same subject? How many? Are they recent works?

In this Information Age, any of us can expand our knowledge of publications with a small amount of research. Although we'll take up marketing later in this book, begin looking for publications or books on the subject areas of your writing. Go online and find more resources there.

RESOURCES FOR DEMOGRAPHICS AND PUBLICATIONS

The Index of Leading Cultural Indicators by William J. Bennett

The American Directory of Writer's Guidelines edited by John C. Mutchler, with 450 magazine and book publishers

Pub List website: www.publist.com, featuring a database of 150,000 magazines, journals, and newsletters

Read potential publications with the specific idea of learning more about your reader. After you have read half a dozen copies of a magazine or journal or half a dozen books, you should have a more clearly defined picture of your reader. In the process, you can't help but absorb some of the publication's diction (manner of speaking), syntax (sentence structure), vocabulary, complexity of ideas and presentation, biases of the writer and publication, and style.

If you plan to write a book, read everything you can about the topic you'll be writing on. Take notes on your study of similar works, because you'll need to describe these books later in a section of the nonfiction book proposal called "About the Competition." In particular, you'll describe how your proposed book is similar to and different from other titles on your subject. Notice whether other authors address the same reader you envision for your book. How do you know this from their writing?

For instance, when I scan a book on writing, I immediately register whether the intended reader is a beginner, apprentice, professional, or all three. From tone and biases, I determine if the writer, and therefore the reader, prefers a no-nonsense business approach or a holistic approach. (My bias runs toward a holistic approach, one that considers the reader as a person who writes rather than as a mammal whose digits produce words.)

Some writers believe that any consideration other than the creative process, especially consideration of a market or audience, must be avoided or the writing itself will be tainted or "less authentic." I think this is oversimplified. The way I see it, there are three kinds of writing: (1) writing for its own sake, (2) writing for its own sake that eventually finds a reader, and (3) writing with a reader in mind. Writing is communication. If I write for my own sake, I'm doing so for a variety of personal reasons. Most of the time, it takes the form of journals, poetry, writing exercises, or brainstorming. Sometimes one of these pieces of self-expression will strike me as having potential, and I'll work with it until it seems suitable for sending out for publication. The very act of determining suitability means that a reader has become involved in the process. Now, writing means communication to *somebody*.

If you write because you wish to be read, it's better to hold your potential reader in mind while you write than to pretend one doesn't exist, as if acknowledging your reader would render your writing less pure. Consciousness of an audience for your work doesn't mean that your writing will be less authentic. In fact, it may be superior because of the conversation you hold with your reader in your mind.

Know thyself. Know thy demographics. Know thy publications.

In the next chapter, you'll learn how to select a form to fit the ideas you want to express.

THREE

What Form Can My Writing Take?

If you want your ship to come in,
you must build the dock.

Anonymous

SHOULD IT BE A sonata or a symphony, a tarantella or a waltz? Just as composers select a form to express a musical idea, writers also select a form to express their literary ideas. If you have a lively melody in your head, you must first know what a tarantella is—it's a fast-paced Italian dance—before you select it. The same is true for writing; first you learn the forms and then you select what suits your purposes.

The dozens of forms of nonfiction writing all stem from three basic forms: articles, essays, and books.

Articles

My Webster's dictionary defines an article as a piece of nonfiction writing that appears in a magazine, newspaper, or book. Essays (which we'll discuss later) also fit this definition, but an article is usually written with objectivity in mind; that is, the writer seeks to report about, and perhaps intellectually interpret, the subject of the article. Writers of articles, in the strictest meaning of the word, omit or minimize their personal experiences, emotions, and realizations. The newspaper, for instance, is about 95 percent articles and 5 percent essays. Articles include news, reports, product descriptions, and profiles of people. Newspaper essays include letters to the editor, commentaries, and travel experiences.

Essays

Essays, unlike articles, intentionally include or even feature the writer's subjective viewpoint and experiences. Besides political and social commentary in newspapers, the essay form encompasses personal experiences of all kinds. Essays are further distinguished from articles by a structure suited to argue an opinion or tell a story. Literary journals and most magazines accept essays and may even include a regular forum for essays in each issue.

DISTINGUISHING AN ARTICLE FROM AN ESSAY

Because the article is the most widespread of all nonfiction forms, the word *article* is often used in a general way that isn't technically accurate. For instance, while writing this chapter, I received a telephone inquiry from a writer asking me about editing her article, a first-person story about her family. As I asked more questions about the piece, it was clear to me that she had written an essay. She could have written an article about her family that included her personal experiences, but the focus, tone, and even content would have been journalistic, like a report. What helped me know it was an essay was her approach; it was subjective and personal.

Occasionally, the line between article and essay blurs so completely as to defy categorization—and it doesn't matter. For instance, an article on cooking, with recipes, might be told from a subjective viewpoint, including vignettes of the writer's life. The same holds true for some cookbooks; they may be works of creative nonfiction as much or more than how-to cookbooks.

Books

What makes a book one of the three forms of nonfiction is not its style of writing but its length. What length defines a book instead of a booklet or simply a very long article? Although the dictionary uses binding as the definition of a book, works exceeding 100 printed pages are typically accepted as books. As you might expect, writing a book is a far more complex affair than what is needed to write an article or essay, and yet, the building blocks of organization are the same.

Variations on the Form

Within these three broad types of nonfiction—articles, essays, and books—several styles and forms exist. You'll need to know how to label your writing to market it correctly, and that requires knowing the conventions of form for each piece you write. We'll discuss how to organize and develop the different types of nonfiction in chapter six. First, however, we'll discuss the names and definitions of the following common nonfiction forms:

- Informational/Educational
- How-to
- Feature
- Profile
- Column
- Opinion
- Personal experience

INFORMATIONAL/EDUCATIONAL

Reports on events and the people involved in them make up the typical news story you read in your daily paper. The "informational article" simply reports about some event, thing, or person of interest. Information stories—news—are the backbone of nonfiction.

Educational writing—in articles, textbooks, or general interest books—represents an enormous portion of all written material.

Four particular kinds of information articles are:

- Investigative/Exposé
- Consumer product
- Consumer service
- Technical

Investigative/Exposé

An in-depth analysis of an issue, investigative articles probe the depth and breadth of a subject with the intent of revealing information that has been kept secret or is not well known. Common subjects of investigative articles are education, politics, welfare, senior citizens, health, safety, consumer fraud, and miscarriages of justice. Although investigative and exposé writers seek to inform the reader, they may also hope to persuade the reader to take action. Often, the subject involves a complex and/or long history and a serious problem. The investigative report dominates broadcast journalism with shows such as *20/20, 48 Hours,* and *60 Minutes.* A superb example of in-depth investigative writing is the book *Fast Food Nation,* by Eric Schlosser, who investigated "the dark side of the all-American meal," tracing the origins of our beef from cow to eatery. An entirely different kind of exposé was Barbara Ehrenreich's book *Nickel and Dimed,* describing what it was like for her to become a member of the working poor.

You may hear the terms "investigative" and "exposé" used interchangeably. However, "investigative" implies open-mindedness to discovery whereas "exposé" assumes wrongdoing from the start and makes the strongest emotional appeal for reform.

Consumer Product

Ideal as "fillers," these very short information articles review products. For instance, a magazine about walking and fitness might include consumer-product pieces on athletic shoes. Science magazines print short articles on inventions and tools, and airline magazines boast consumer-product pieces about laptops and personal-assistant software.

Consumer service

Like consumer-product pieces, consumer-service articles are, in essence, information plus a review. But in this case, the review is about a service such as massage, mail delivery, or home health care. A specialized form of consumer-service writing is the artistic review—of movies, musical performances, dance, and visual art, to name a few of the most common types.

Technical

The words *employed* and *writer* seldom make their way into one sentence. What associations pop into your mind for the phrase "employed writer" (besides oxymoron)? I think most of us would say "reporter" or perhaps "staff writer" for a magazine, but "technical writer" may pay better and employ more writers than the prior two.

Technical writing is a form of information and how-to writing that describes "processes" in detail. Although you may associate technical writing with the burgeoning field of consumer electronics and their manuals, other industries—such as government, the educational and research institutions, and private and public corporations—rely on technical articles.

Just think of all the specifications that must be clearly described on contracts that go out to bidders. Think of the proposals for grants that bidders must submit to compete for contracts. Technical writing keeps business doing business.

HOW-TO

I don't think it would be an overstatement to say that our culture is obsessed with how to do *everything,* and we turn to articles and books to help us. We're literate, we have expendable funds, and we live in a relatively stable society. We also enjoy being consumers and share a mythos of can-do confidence. The happy result for a writer of how-to pieces is truly an inexhaustible market.

As instructional pieces, how-to articles and books cover the visible and the invisible world we live in, both the physical and nonphysical worlds.

Subcategories of how-to writing include:

- Technical
- Self-help
- Inspirational

Technical

At one time, technical how-to material served a workplace market more than a consumer market. However, we all seem to be "dummies" and "idiots" who ingest these books like M&Ms. I date the shift of style in how-to literature from traditional instructional style to a technical-writing style with our global entry into the computer era, and our reliance on the Internet in particular. This information revolution popularized technical writing, which facilitates quick access of information better than any other how-to writing. I made a decision in the mid-nineties to use technical-writing conventions for all of my instructional books for writers, beginning with my first book, *Nonfiction Book Proposals Anybody Can Write*. Although the "dummy," "idiots," and "everything" books feature technical-writing style, they are often poor examples of it. Other non-series how-to books are good examples of technical writing, such as *How to Profit by Forming Your Own Limited Liability Company*, by Scott E. Friedman, *How to Publish and Promote Online*, by M. J. Rose and Angela Adair-Hoy, and *Rich Dad's Loopholes of the Rich*, by Diane Kennedy, CPA.

Self-Help

Self-help articles and books about intangible subjects cover relationships, spiritual matters, and intellectual processes. This self-help writing makes a particular kind of promise: empowerment of the reader. You can easily identify the self-help form of how-to because you can recognize the promised benefit of improvement: managing anger, losing weight, or communicating with a boss, all typical self-help subjects.

Inspirational

Most of the time, the inspirational how-to article addresses spirituality and religion. However, it can be motivational without any religion or spirituality, such as the book *Who Moved My Cheese?*, by Dr. Spencer Johnson. Writing fits this category as motivational rather than spiritual if it offers its readers specific steps to improve themselves and at the same time is "uplifting." All of Wayne Dyer's books, such as *Real Magic* and *Your Sacred Self*, are examples of uplifting but nonreligious, inspirational writing. Psychologist Al Siebert's *The Survival Personality* is more psychological and not as "spiritual," but is both helpful in a practical sense and inspirational.

FEATURE

A "feature" is an article with a human-interest angle. Its purpose goes beyond news and information. A feature engages its readers in the story of people or of a single person behind a newsworthy event. This means that well-written features are meant to arouse emotions. The writer might accomplish this through humor, for instance, or by conveying the emotions of the people involved in the event. A feature of a politician brings laughs as the writer describes how he scoops the you-know-what behind the horses in his hometown's fall celebration parade. A feature about a star athlete who was killed by a drunk driver brings tears. Further, the way you write a feature can depart from strict journalistic writing and may borrow techniques from fiction.

> **RESOURCES ON FEATURE WRITING**
>
> *Writing for Story*
> by Jon Franklin
> *The Complete Book of Feature Writing*
> edited by Leonard Witt

PROFILE

This form focuses on a single individual or, occasionally, on a related group. A profile may be a feature, but in the strictest sense of the word, a profile does not require a newsworthy event like a feature does. There may not be a news "peg" or "tie-in," meaning a recent and relevant bit of news. Sometimes referred to as "personality profiles," the subject of a profile is newsworthy because he or she is noteworthy.

Profiles may feature celebrities or noncelebrities. They may cover people in interesting jobs and careers or people with unusual hobbies and pastimes. Nearly every newspaper and magazine welcomes a well-written profile.

Q&A or Interview

Not fitting the definition of an information article, feature, or profile, the Q&A supplies *questions*—Q—asked by a writer and *answers*—A—supplied by an authority on a subject from politics and current affairs to beauty and sex. This form is also referred to as the "interview article" and relies heavily upon direct quotations. It also requires research and savvy listening and interviewing skills.

COLUMN

Columns are short articles or essays written on one broad subject by one writer. Subjects can be as diverse as politics, sports, nostalgia, health, or writing. The purpose of a given column depends on the columnist and the subject. The writer may wish to entertain, inform, inspire, persuade, or accomplish several of these purposes. Newspaper columns may be as short as 350–500 words, while magazine columns might reach 1000 words. When a columnist offers a report about a "dry" subject, such as household cleaners, his or her voice and personality lend color to the piece and keep the reader riveted to the outcome of the wood-polish debate. That's why columns include bylines (telling who has written the piece) and why they sometimes include the photo or caricature of the writer.

Columns appear daily, monthly, or quarterly depending upon the publication's needs, and they may be syndicated. This means that a corporation called a "syndicate" distributes the columns to other media throughout the country (or world) and pays the author of the column a percentage of the sale.

Most columns fit the definition of an essay because they offer the subjective views of the columnist. Every opinion-editorial section of the newspaper has regular columns by political analysts such as Molly Ivins, William Safire, and Norman Solomon. The advice column *Dear Abby* is an institution.

OPINION

Sharing characteristics of informative and investigative articles, opinion essays offer the writer's opinion—intellectual, emotional, or both. The shortest form of an opinion piece is the "letter to the editor," an opportunity open to writers and nonwriters alike for publication and self-expression. "Editorials" are longer essays than letters to the editor, but they are staff written with the exception of "guest editorials." "Commentaries" are opinion essays usually written by experts on a particular subject. Columns can likewise be opinion essays. More developed opinion pieces are often organized to meet the development of a formal argument that posits a thesis and uses inductive or deductive reasoning and evidence.

PERSONAL EXPERIENCE

The most common type of personal-experience nonfiction is an account of an extraordinary or unique event in the narrator's life, what I've coined as "the dramatic and the traumatic." Usually written in first person, these pieces strike an intimate tone and offer a chronological replay of the events, including novelistic descriptions of setting and people, remembered or re-created dialogue, and dramatic story structure. The writer of personal-experience nonfiction may seek to fulfill any of the four purposes: to entertain, inform, inspire, or persuade.

Personal-experience nonfiction is a rich and fulfilling form of writing with many subcategories:

- As Told To
- Confession
- Inspiration
- Nostalgia
- Humor

- Memoir
- Autobiography
- Biography/Family History

As Told To

A personal experience is an "as told to" when someone other than the person who had the experience does the writing. Usually written in first person, these essays retain the intimacy and voice of the narrator. Sometimes the writer of the piece is acknowledged with a byline that reads "as told to" or "with" (which can imply some cowriting), and other times the story is "ghosted" without acknowledgment to the writer. A good example involves naturalist Tom Brown Jr., who was catapulted into the limelight with his bestselling book *The Tracker,* as told to William Jon Watkins. Interestingly, his next book, *The Search*, shows a byline of "Tom Brown Jr. with William Owen." For his third book, *The Vision,* his byline is in big letters *above* the title, and if he used a ghostwriter, he is invisible— no credit given.

Confession

These articles are allegedly true experiences, related in a confidential manner, confessing the wrongdoings, shortcomings, and private matters of the first-person writer. Confession articles convey everyday challenges, the ordinary rather than the extraordinary. Subjects include marital indiscretions, sexual inadequacies, matters of love and loss, and problems with children, relatives, and neighbors. The purpose of confessions may be to reform more than to inform, since the narrator typically "comes to realize" a moral truth. It is widely known that many writers create these stories to practice their fiction-writing skills.

Inspiration

Inspirational, personal-experience nonfiction differs from the inspirational how-to in several ways. It seeks to inspire and uplift through true-life stories rather than to inform through specific instructional points. Two of the best-known general-interest magazines featuring inspirational essays are *Reader's Digest* and

Guideposts. This kind of writing often has a religious message or scriptural source for the inspiration, but it may also simply be heart-warming like the popular *Chicken Soup* or *Cup of Comfort* series.

Nostalgia

Everyone has a different idea of what constitutes the "good old days," but most of us like to reminisce. Nostalgic nonfiction focuses on the unique "characters," lifestyles, culture, work lives, language, and everyday objects of a particular year or era. The emotional tone is light and the purpose is usually to entertain.

Humor

Humor writers mine their personal experiences for material. They may tell a story using narrative techniques, or they may relate personal experiences to make a point and offer an opinion. Humor writers gain a lot of help in craft by learning how to structure jokes, work with timing, and deliver punch lines. Many humor writers take lessons in stand-up comedy to improve their writing!

Memoir

This book-length treatment of the personal-experience story can be inspirational, nostalgic, confessional, as-told-to, or literary. The memoir is not the same as autobiography. It recounts a time period or set of experiences in the author's life that illustrates a single theme. In the past, noteworthy, newsworthy, and notorious people dominated the form of the memoir. However, about a decade ago, memoirs by unknown authors burst on the scene and were supported by the buying public. Bestsellers are testimony to the support by the buying public, memoirs such as *Angela's Ashes*, by Frank McCourt, and *Into Thin Air*, by Jon Krakauer. The market remains open to the experienced writer with a story to tell. The travel memoir, in particular, has emerged as a recognized subcategory of the memoir.

Autobiography

In contrast to memoirs, autobiographies span the life of the author. These book-length stories typically progress chronologically, often beginning with childhood and continuing to the author's present age. Celebrity autobiographies—or those written by a person of acknowledged fame, accomplishment, or historical significance—dominate the field. Occasionally, an autobiography of a noncelebrity emerges, such as the three books by Dave Pelzer. His first book—which became a bestseller—was *A Child Called "It,"* recounting how he survived abuse by his mother. He followed this book with *The Lost Boy,* describing his foster home experiences, and finished his autobiography with *A Man Named Dave,* revealing how he has come to terms with his life experiences as an adult.

Biography/Family History

The biography is a book-length presentation of an accomplished or noteworthy individual. Many successful biographies have been published detailing the lives of notables, such as Charles Lindbergh (*An American Hero*), Edna St. Vincent Millay (*Savage Beauty*), and John Forbes Nash (*A Beautiful Mind*). When a family member writes about a relative or ancestor, he or she is writing a "family history." Both the biography and the family history offer information, insight, and often entertainment. Biographies need not always be about people! Consider the bestseller *Seabiscuit,* by Laura Hillenbrand, about the racehorse who won the Triple Crown. Many biographies inspire as much as inform. Although written in third person, they often resemble memoir and autobiography by recounting the dramatic and fascinating events in the life of the subject.

From Form to Organization

Every art has form, and that form has requirements and restrictions. Landscape, portrait, seascape, and still life are each different artistic forms. If you're going to paint a landscape, you'd better know about perspective. If you plan to do a portrait, you'll draw a very odd face if you don't understand how to block out its sections or how far apart to place the eyes.

In the next chapter, you'll learn how to organize your writing and which method of organization makes a good match with each of the forms and categories of writing mentioned in this chapter. For future reference, Map 3-1 summarizes the forms and categories of nonfiction writing.

MAP 3-1

The Many Forms of Nonfiction

THREE BASIC FORMS: Articles, Essays, Books

CATEGORIES & SUBCATEGORIES

> INFORMATIONAL/EDUCATIONAL
>> Investigative/Exposé
>> Consumer product
>> Consumer service
>> Technical

> HOW-TO
>> Technical
>> Self-help
>> Inspirational

> FEATURE

> PROFILE
>> Q&A

> COLUMN

> OPINION

> PERSONAL EXPERIENCE
>> As Told To
>> Confession
>> Inspiration
>> Nostalgia
>> Humor
>> Memoir
>> Autobiography
>> Biography/Family History

FOUR

How Can I Refine My Idea?

The process of discovery is very simple. An unwearied and systematic application of known laws to nature causes the unknown to reveal themselves.

Henry David Thoreau

MANY WRITERS MAKE THE mistake of sailing directly into writing. They've completed their research, they know their purpose and audience, and they're eager to begin. What else is necessary? Without giving thought to a slant or organization of ideas, they're putting all bets on lady luck. Sometimes she comes through, but more often, there are rough seas ahead. By taking the time to chart your course in advance, you'll have a better idea of where you're heading with your writing—or where it's taking you.

Slant

Slant is the perspective from which you approach your subject. Picking the right slant can increase the power of the hook and allow you to better reach your reader. In fact, to make a play on words, think of yourself as an "angler." In this case, you're going fishing for readers. You have a subject that you want to share. Perhaps you believe you know something your readers need. The subject and need alone may not prove enough lure in a competitive marketplace to make readers select your article or book. You need to target your writing to the reader you want to attract.

Because fish have different taste buds, not all of them will lick their lips over worms or eggs. In fact, some prefer colorful flys over such fine delectables. Slant not only depends on what will lure your reader to the hook, it also depends on what you are writing. Anglers need the proper bait. Slant is bait.

Slants fall into common types. The first place to detect a slant is in a title. As you read magazine articles and books, even if only their titles, identify the slant according to the following list. If you find a slant not on this list, add it! When you begin writing a piece, create a title that reflects the slant you choose, even if you decide to change it later when you revise. Also know that it is unlikely that your working title will be retained by the publication that buys your writing. In essence, your title is a homing beacon for your slant.

Types of Slant

The fifteen most common slants are:

- Adrenaline
- Amazement
- Brand-New
- Detailed
- Funny
- Location
- Money
- Newsy
- Numbers
- Promises
- Secrets
- Sexy
- Superlatives
- Unexpected
- Combination

ADRENALINE

Any piece of writing that gets the blood rushing—out of fear, anger, or excitement—is an adrenaline slant. Why, you might ask, would any decent writer want to make a reader afraid or angry? We live in a world of grave problems. Fear and anger shake people out of their complacency. That's a great way for a writer to make a difference. On the other hand, getting adrenaline flowing over something exciting and positive also reflects this slant.

Read the following actual titles and you'll sense the adrenaline slant. Consider the arousal of fear and anger implied in these three titles, which appeared in the same issue of *Audubon* magazine: "Lost!," "Perilous Crossing," and "A Habitat Held Hostage." The emotion of fear or anger can be implied and used in a subtle way for a subject that is not about physical survival. An example is "Safety Net" with the descriptive line, "How to dodge the perils of online research," by E. A. Vander Veer in *The Writer*. A title and book that increases my heartbeat is *Running with Scissors,* by Augusten Burroughs. What's it about? It's a memoir about a psychiatrist who went crazy.

AMAZEMENT

Rather than get adrenaline flowing, this slant is more likely to get conversation flowing—"Hey, Maude, get a load of this." You may be writing about something that is unusual or even freakish, though probably not as freakish as supermarket rags that shout, "Woman Gives Birth to 50-Pound Gorilla." A title that hooks the reader by creating amazement may be accurate about a totally respectable subject such as "How the Universe Will End," a title on the cover of one *Time* magazine.

BRAND-NEW

I have used the label "brand-new" rather than simply "new" to distinguish it from the slant about information called "newsy." Brand-new is the perfect slant for writing about discoveries, innovations, the cutting edge, or simply about a new spin. Examples: "The New American Family," by Stephen Phillip Policoff in *New Age,* or "The New Love Triangle," by Dr. Evan Imber-Black in *New Woman* introducing technology as the new mistress that steals intimacy from relationships. Notice, too, how many magazines use the "new" hook in their names—*New Woman, New Age, New Choices.*

DETAILED

When a subject has been so well canvassed that all of the other slants have been used and used again, you may only get your reader's attention by using a highly detailed slant. For instance, everything under the sun has already been said about gardening or visiting Puerto Vallarta. You may not be able to find anyone interested in general subjects like "Summer Vegetable Gardening" or "Sunsets in Puerto Vallarta." You may have to be even more detailed to guarantee uniqueness. Perhaps a title such as "Fire Pit Roasting of Summer Corn" or "Karaoke, Puerto Vallarta Style" will do the trick.

FUNNY

If you can make your readers smile and laugh, that is a slant all its own. You can see how any subject is altered by the addition of humor, how comedy adds sufficient bait to lure readers. The following title of a book made me smile: *Do Not Talk to, Touch, Marry, or Otherwise Fiddle with Frogs,* by Nailah Shami.

LOCATION

It may seem strange to you, but location or locale can be your best slant. I own many books on feng shui, but I bought one because its title addressed my next project, *Feng Shui for Your Office.* The slant was determined by the location. Here are some other slants from location-based titles: "Internet Pets: Dog Sites on the Web," by Staci Veitch, and "Capitol Dogs," by Ridings and White, both in *Animal Advocate.*

MONEY

You know you've seen a zillion articles that use the money slant. Why? Because we are all interested in getting money, holding on to it, and spending it. If your material involves any aspect of money, put the slant in your title and develop the piece along those lines. Examples: "Stashing Cash at Home," by Marc Myers in *Reader's Digest;* "Stake Your Claim to Wealth," by staff in *Fortune Technology Guide.*

NEWSY

Most of the articles in the newspaper, in newsletters, and in academic or technical publications have a newsy slant. In fact, this slant lends itself best to newspapers, web sites, and publications that are part of the "immediate media." In this slant, the subject itself is the slant. From one newspaper, here are but a few of the newsy slants: "Deeper U.S. Deficit Predicted," "Bingo Parlor Sues Over Smoking Ban," or "Israel Presses Gaza Assault."

NUMBERS

When you're stuck for a slant, see if numbers will work. Nearly every magazine has at least one article that features a numbers slant. We seem to love counting steps—three, seven, ten; time—days, months, years; processes—ways or points. Take the articles "24 Hours, Zero Stress," by M. P. Dunleavey, and "Beauty Spree! 93 New Hair, Skin, Makeup Finds," by staff, both in *New Woman.* Equally popular in book titles, the number slant shows up frequently, for example: *The 7 Habits of Highly Effective People,* by Stephen Covey, or *Seven Secrets of a Happy Marriage,* by Margery Rosen and the editors of *Ladies' Home Journal.*

PROMISES

If a reader has a need and you can provide a solution, you'll find no better bait than a promise slant. Most women's, self-help, and fitness magazines include at least one article each month that uses a promises slant: "Eat Well, Live Longer," by Walter C. Willett, M.D., in *New Age,* or "Reverse Your Memory Loss" and "Total Recall," by Underwood and Watson, as reprinted in *Reader's Digest.*

Books also reflect the promises slant, such as *Healing Digestive Disorders,* by Andrew Gaeddert, or *How to Be Ageless: Growing Better, Not Just Older!,* by Suzy Allegra. But writer beware: Never promise something you can't deliver.

SECRETS

Curiosity is the basis of this slant. Can you stand to have one of your friends whisper a secret to another friend and not want to know what they are talking about? This is a powerful slant *if* your reader cares about the subject enough to want the inside scoop, the untold story. Consider this title: "The Northern Lights: The True Story of the Man Who Unlocked the Secrets of the Aurora Borealis," by Lucy Jago in *The World & I.* An entirely different use of the secrets slant is reflected in these titles: "Secrets of Successful Fat Burning," by Malissa Thompson in *New Woman;* or "Hidden Treasures: Techniques to Help You Find the Essence of Your Poem," by Rachel Hadas in *The Writer.*

SEXY

No writer with integrity would use sex as a slant, right? Wrong. A sexy slant doesn't have to be sleazy, especially about plant propagation or how chocolate increases pheromone production. You don't have to use words that would make Dr. Ruth blush. Innuendo can be a great sexy slant. Courting disaster? This writer didn't think so: "Suddenly Sex: 21 No-Fail Firestarters," by Hagar Scher in *New Woman.* The bestseller *The Botany of Desire* made me want to run out and buy it because I'm a plant lover. What's it about? It describes how angiosperms (the flowering plants) prosper by seducing other creatures, including upright mammals.

SUPERLATIVES

When we share our enthusiasm with others over a restaurant, hotel, vacation, golf course, or favorite book, we often gush with superlatives: "It was the best enchilada." "They had fine service." "It was the most challenging class." Any word that implies a sweeping evaluation, such as richest, poorest, largest, smallest, best, worst, is a superlative that can supply this slant. Examples include "Dream Hair," by Carol Straley in *Ladies' Home Journal,* or "Total Recall," by Rothman Morris in *Working Mother.* Two favorite superlatives that slant book titles are the words "best" and "greatest": *The Best Small Towns in America,* by Norman Crampton, or *The Best Spiritual Writing 2002,* edited by Philip Zaleski; *The Greatest Firefighter Stories Never Told,* by Allan Zullo, Mara Bovsun, and Mike Santangelo.

UNEXPECTED

Readers love surprises. An unexpected idea or unusual viewpoint will intrigue and surprise them. "Chocolate Is Good for You." I knew that, did you? Sometimes a writer may want to take the "devil's advocate" role and challenge a prevailing viewpoint, such as *Die Broke,* by Pollan and Levine, or he may believe strongly in an unpopular viewpoint such as "Human Beings, Not Animals, Are the Endangered Species." Here are some titles that use an unexpected slant: "The Anti-Diet: Eat What You Love and Lose," the cover title on a *Ladies' Home Journal* issue for an article entitled, "I Stopped Dieting—and Lost Weight," by Michelle Stacey.

COMBINATION

Can you use more than one slant in your title and lead? Definitely, as long as you don't confuse your reader by losing your primary hook. For instance, a title such as "The Ten Best Nightclubs in New York" combines three slants: numbers, superlatives, and location. Take any one of the three slants away and you have a dull or incomplete slant.

Titles

When you have figured out what slant or slants might work for your material, create your "working title." This is how professional writers refer to titles that may later be changed or to communicate their openness to changing a title in a query letter.

A great title can sell a piece, or nearly so. It can at least make an editor or agent take a closer look at your writing. Scribble down any title that comes to mind that reflects both your slant and your subject. When you have brainstormed a good, long list, stop. A good title involves yet other considerations.

Every magazine, for instance, favors a particular style of title over others. You'll increase your chance of selling an article or essay if your style matches that of the publication. All you need to do is study the titles of the magazines where you wish to place your writing. You'll quickly see a pattern. Some favor one-word or two-word titles. Some always use "two-parters," a primary title followed by a subtitle. Other magazines use gerunds—a noun with an "ing" ending, such as "swimming," "eating," or "saving." I remember reading one magazine where the titles got to be a bit much, too kitschy; all of them rhymed, something like "Fishy Dishes," or "Sporty Courting." An occasional rhyming title adds poetic power as in "Flower Power," by Daryn Eller in *Victoria.* I've also seen magazines that use nothing but alliteration in their titles—"Crushed Cherry Crepes" or "Fine Festive Fruits." Pardon the pun, but use good taste when you select your titles.

About thirty thousand nonfiction books are published each year in the United States. That's a lot of titles. However, if you study the titles that match your subject area, you'll begin to see a pattern. With exceptions, most book titles are five words or under, although their subtitles may be longer. Most of the time, the subject of the book must be clear from the main title and not hidden in the subtitle. Book titles will frequently display one of the fourteen slants, but they may use the promise to the reader. In the terminology of finding book titles, the "promise" represents the strongest selling slant. The "promise" as applied to book-length nonfiction is commonly referred to as the reader "benefit," what the reader yearns for but doesn't have. Examples of benefits include losing weight, gaining self-esteem, increasing understanding, or being entertained. If your title can answer the question "What will my reader get?" you've captured a promise or benefit slant.

Titles for creative, or literary, nonfiction essays and books are often evocative. This means they are poetic or mysterious and allude to rather than explicitly tell what the piece is about. Evocative titles do seek to create a particular mood or reflect the yearning of the story promise, such as these titles: *The Danger Tree, Boswell's Presumptuous Task,* or *Chasing the Hawk.*

Often, we writers cannot think of a good title until after we've written our articles, essays, or books. A working title is still a good idea, even if it is not "the one." As long as you're clear about your purpose, promise, the difference you wish to make, and your slant, you can write your piece without a firm title.

With a slant and a working title, you're truly ready to write your first words. "Well begun is half done," said Aristotle. And it will be—after you know everything there is to know about leads.

FIVE

How Do I Begin?

You cannot cross the sea merely
by standing and staring at the water.
R. Tagore

BEGINNING IS ONE of the most difficult things we human beings do, whether we're talking about putting on athletic shoes and heading out the door for a walk, or sweeping and mopping the kitchen floor, or typing the first words on blank paper. My guess is that half of the difficulty of beginning is making the commitment. The other half is confidence, and confidence makes committing to a piece of writing less difficult. But where or how do you get confidence? I believe it is a direct result of building skill, and skill is based on knowledge and practice. Once a writer knows how to begin a piece, and after that how to develop it, much of the resistance to beginning vanishes.

Beginning

The first sentence or the first few paragraphs are called the "lead" or "opening." The length of a lead depends on what kind of non-fiction you intend to write. The lead may be as short as a single sentence or as long as a chapter. Most of the time, the lead for an article or essay includes just the first paragraph.

Like the slant, the foremost purpose of a lead is to hook the reader's attention. How a writer grabs his reader depends on many factors: his purpose in writing, his audience, how he wishes to make a difference, the promise, and what emotional reaction he seeks to make. If this sounds like a big job, it is. But it's an all-important job for insuring that the sweat of your labor gets read! With practice, juggling all of these requirements will, I promise, become second nature.

The style and tone of a lead depend on what you are writing. Despite all of these variables, standard *types* of leads have been well mapped and include at least fifteen common options.

- Analogy or Comparison
- Anecdotal or Case History
- Combination
- Direct Address
- Factual
- Journalistic
- Metaphor
- Descriptive or Narrative
- One-Line Hook
- Question
- Quotation
- Controversial
- Statistical
- Summary
- Thematic

An example and brief analysis of each of these fifteen types follows. We'll discuss how each lead reveals the writer's purpose, the audience, and the promise. In addition, I'll describe how I think the writer demonstrates making a difference and what emotional reaction each lead evokes in me. Your reactions may differ from mine and are equally valid.

ANALOGY OR COMPARISON

You might think that the difference between analogy and comparison is splitting hairs. And in a way it is, because analogy is a form of comparison. An analogy affirms similarities by comparing two strikingly different things. A comparison includes similarities and/ or differences. Consider this analogy lead:

In the past, searching for a lost pet was like throwing a dart in the dark. Regardless of the effort—the flyers posted, the ads taken out in the newspaper, and the visits to the animal shelter—the chances of hitting the bull's-eye and finding a lost pet depended mostly on luck. ("No Longer a Shot in the Dark," by Catherine M. Rosenthal in *Animal Advocate*)

Analysis: The "strikingly different things" being compared here are "searching" to "throwing darts in the dark" and "finding a lost pet" to "hitting a bull's-eye." The result of an analogy is a clearer sense of *similarity,* but notice how colorful the comparisons are.

Here is one more analogy, the lead to a column, "Crisis in the Critique Group—Part I," that I wrote for a newsletter. (The full column is also posted on my website: www.elizabethlyon.com.)

A bad critique group is like being lost in the TV show *A Nightmare on Elm Street*. A good critique group is like a best friend. But a great group is like soaring with the eagles.

Analysis: The "strikingly different" and "colorful" analogies to a bad, good, and great critique group are a TV show, a best friend, and soaring with the eagles.

The next lead to chapter two in *How to Profit by Forming Your Own Limited Liability Company,* by Scott E. Friedman, is a comparison lead.

Limited liability companies (LLCs) combine the flexibility and tax advantages of partnerships with the limited liability features of corporations. At the same time, they eliminate all restrictions on ownership, as well as legal restrictions on active participation by its owners, and they can be tailored to maximize the operational flexibility of the business.

Analysis: This lead compares the similarities of LLCs with partnerships and corporations, yet it also points out the differences between LLCs and corporations. The language is anything but colorful; in fact, rather than being evocative, the language is literal.

ANECDOTAL OR CASE HISTORY

One of the most popular leads—anecdotes or case histories—create an immediate bond with the reader through the lead's human-interest appeal. The people featured in an effective anecdote may be fictional or real, but they should reflect the demographics of your reader. Fictional anecdotes may be based on real-life people and situations. True anecdotes or case histories often use fictional names to protect the identities of the actual people (and the author from lawsuit!).

> One rainy Saturday morning after reading an article in a magazine about the "Ten Best Places to Pick Up Your Next Boyfriend and Make Him Instantly Fall for You," thirty-two-year-old Jane doused herself with her newly arrived pheromone spray and bounced off to the grocery store to meet her next beloved. As she rounded the corner to the produce section, she almost had a head-on cart collision with The One, who was plunking a bunch of bananas into his cart. (*Do Not Talk to, Touch, Marry, or Otherwise Fiddle with Frogs: How to Find Prince Charming by Finding Yourself,* by Nailah Shami)

Analysis: Purpose: to entertain. Reader: single women under forty. Difference made: to get readers to change their behavior. Promise: hope. Emotional reaction: laughs.

The anecdotal/case history lead, because it introduces a real or fictitious person with a problem, is a favorite for beginning how-to and self-help articles:

> Janice was upset and embarrassed. She frequently forgot appointments, and sometimes, in the middle of a sentence, she forgot what she was going to say. Only fifty-eight years old, Janice worried that she was in the first throes of Alzheimer's disease. (*The Memory Cure,* by Thomas H. Crook III, Ph.D., and Brenda Adderly, M.H.A.)

Analysis: Purpose: to engage; to inform. Reader: women more than men, age fifty and older. Difference made: to improve memory. Promise: reverse fears. Emotional reaction: empathy—a me-too feeling.

COMBINATION

Often, your choice of lead will turn out to be a combination of several leads. No problem. Consider the following lead for a first-person essay. It combines a quotation, descriptive, and metaphor lead.

> The right road is always a problem, as Dante reminds us in the opening line of *The Inferno,* and there is no end of ways to lose it. The summer I turned fifty, I began to wonder exactly when the right path had turned into such a deep rut. The problem, in my case, was that the dark woods had become entirely metaphoric— too many years at the same job, mortgage payments, a minivan!— while the real woods of my youth now seemed a lost world. (*Audubon,* "Lost," by John Hildebrand)

Analysis: Purpose: to entertain. Reader: men and women who enjoy the outdoors. Difference made: to recall times of being lost in life and to gain the necessary insight to find the right road once again. Promise: insight. Emotional reaction: identification with author.

DIRECT ADDRESS

Direct address means that *you* address the reader by using the second person—"you." It's fine to combine direct address with the use of another lead.

> Almost every religion on earth accepts the fact that our spirits survive death. But tell people you can communicate with those spirits, and they will think you are nuts. So spirits exist, but we can't communicate with them? I think *that's* nuts! Of course we can, and we do it all the time, whether we are aware of it or not. (*The Other Side and Back: A Psychic's Guide to Our World and Beyond,* by Sylvia Browne)

Analysis: Purpose: to persuade. Reader: anyone interested in metaphysics and spirituality, probably more women then men. Difference made: to replace readers' doubt with faith. Promise: validation, comfort, security. Emotional reaction: curiosity.

In this next example of a direct-address lead, notice how the "you" is more personal than the collective "you" used in the previous example.

> New moms have it harder today. You probably live far from your childhood home and don't have the same network of support. . . . Yet, as a first-time mom, you need help and emotional support more than ever. (*The New Mom's Manual,* by Mary Jeanne Menna)

Analysis: Purpose: to inform and support. Reader: mothers of babies one year or younger. Difference made: to create good parents and healthy babies. Promise: security and confidence. Emotional reaction: relief, comfort. Sense of not being alone.

FACTUAL

Factual leads can be specific—chock-full of facts—or they may be general, leaving development and support of their general statements to the body of the article. Here is a specific, factual lead:

> Having pioneered the multimedia PDA, Casio ups the ante with the stylish EM-500. (*Fortune Technology Guide*)

Analysis: Purpose: to inform. Reader: young adult through age fifty, men more than women. Difference made: to empower to make a best choice when buying a "personal digital assistant." Promise: satisfaction. Emotional reaction: excitement, curiosity.

Here is an example of a general, factual lead:

> For birders, Florida has always been full of surprises, adventures, and great bird sightings. (Tony Tedeschi in *Audubon*)

Analysis: Purpose: to inform and persuade readers to visit. Reader: birders. Difference made: to increase knowledge of birds and to continue to support their protection. Promise: to add many birds to the lifetime list. Emotional reaction: curiosity and anticipation.

JOURNALISTIC

This type of lead crams as much information into the lead as possible. You may have heard of the "Five Ws": who, what, where, when, why. When all of the necessary information about a news story occurs in the lead, an editor can cut everything after that if he needs to do so for space considerations. This explains why the journalistic lead is also called an "hourglass" or "inverted pyramid" lead.

Consider this journalistic lead and the analysis that follows. I've identified the Ws in brackets.

> On October 8, just a few minutes after 3:00 p.m. London time [when/where], more than 10,000 chess fans simultaneously exhaled as Garry Kasparov [who] pushed his king's pawn forward two spaces [how], officially beginning the BrainGames.net World Chess Championship [the primary what]. (*Fortune Technology Guide*)

Analysis: Purpose: to inform. Audience: all ages interested in chess. Difference made: to get readers to explore virtual game sites. Promise: create wonder. Emotional reaction: excitement or appreciation.

We tend to think of this lead as being the province of newspapers alone. However, it can be used for articles, essays, and books as well. Note the different style of this journalistic lead paragraph:

> Thousands of years ago [when], the Toltec [who] were known throughout southern Mexico [where] as "women and men of knowledge [what]." Anthropologists have spoken of the Toltec as a nation or race, but, in fact, the Toltec were scientists and artists who formed a society to explore and conserve the spiritual knowledge and practices of the ancient ones [why]. They came together as masters (*nagual*) and students [how] at Teotihuacan, the ancient city of pyramids outside Mexico City [where] known as the place

where "Man Becomes God." (*The Four Agreements,* by Don Miguel Ruiz)

Analysis: Purpose: to inform but perhaps also to inspire. Audience: any adult interested in anthropology, philosophy, and spirituality. Difference made: implied from the lead but may be transformation through learning about the Toltec knowledge and practices. Promise: again, the promise, like the difference made, is not overt from the lead alone. The book's subtitle reveals the promise: *A Practical Guide to Personal Freedom.* Emotional reaction: for me, the lead creates intrigue and anticipation of learning something that was hitherto secret.

METAPHOR

This less common lead is difficult to write well because metaphors are often brainteasers for writers. A metaphor is a figure of speech that uses one word or phrase to imply another. As a lead, the metaphor must be an apt substitute for the idea you want to express or you will lead the reader down a blind alley.

> The fire of mythology is not easily extinguished, as its flame is fueled from the inexhaustible well of the human psyche. Though we modern humans pay scant heed to the call of myth, we are nonetheless moved by its power. (*The Hero with an African Face: Mythic Wisdom of Traditional Africa,* by Clyde W. Ford)

Analysis: Purpose: to inform and inspire. Reader: lovers of mythology and cultures. Difference made: to encourage connection to mythology in a personal, not just intellectual, way. Promise: to increase one's sense of belonging to the family of man. Emotional reaction: excitement of imminent discovery.

> Metaphors pepper our daily speech and add spice to individual expression.

DESCRIPTIVE OR NARRATIVE

Descriptive or narrative leads tell a story. They are similar to the anecdotal/case history lead, but the descriptive lead differs by not focusing on a "case study" or personal problem. The descriptive or narrative lead is the most common lead used in essays, memoirs, nostalgia pieces, and autobiographies.

Some descriptive or narrative leads focus on description and setting and others focus on events and people. They may be written in first person or third person. They are favored for literary nonfiction, also referred to as "creative nonfiction."

> In early November, snow muffled the Teton Range, forcing the elk down into the valley and a sudden intimacy on all of us. Outside, a whisper worked in place of a shout and the great peaks had fresh personality, bold and showy in the coat of the coming season. It was that best of all times to be breathing air at eight thousand feet in the Rockies; the few weeks when life is on the cusp of doing something else and the money has yet to arrive and put everything out of balance. (*Lasso the Wind,* by Timothy Egan)

Analysis: Purpose: to entertain, and provoke thought. Reader: thoughtful adults who love lyrical yet passionate prose, readers interested in the West and history. Difference made: to feel a sense of place. Promise: to appreciate the environment, both natural and man-made. Emotional reaction: captured, eager to read on.

Egan used a first-person narrative lead in his memoir. Consider the next descriptive lead, written in omniscient third-person.

> A soft fall rain slips down through the trees and the smell of ocean is so strong that it can almost be licked off the air. Trucks rumble along Rogers Street and men in t-shirts stained with fishblood shout to each other from the decks of boats. Beneath them the ocean swells up against the black pilings and sucks back down to the barnacles. (*The Perfect Storm,* by Sebastian Junger)

Analysis: Purpose: to entertain. Reader: probably college-educated because of the book's level of detail and diction. Difference made: to remember the event and the people. Promise: to create awe. Emotional reaction: feeling the menace and power of the ocean.

Descriptive or narrative leads may introduce people and events instead of, or in addition to, settings. Consider this lead for an essay by a mother writing about a son who suffers muscular dystrophy:

> At the Center for Creative Photography, in Tucson, Arizona, my husband, Joe, and I are looking at prints of *Moonrise Hernandez, New Mexico,* by Ansel Adams. A slender young man in a suit has brought us, as requested, three versions of this famous photograph. . . . But that does not change the essential meaning of the photograph, a meaning one never forgets in the Southwest: Nature dominates. Human life is small, fragile, and finite. And yet, still beautiful. ("Moonrise," by Penny Wolfson in *The Atlantic Monthly*)

Analysis: Purpose: to inspire. Reader: parents, especially of children with special needs, educators. Difference made: to break stereotypes. Promise: deeper understanding and compassion. Emotional reaction: appreciation of the preciousness of the moment.

ONE-LINE HOOK

An effective one-line hook is like an arrow hitting a bull's-eye. It can be very difficult to craft because writing short and powerful is always more difficult than writing long. The one-line hook works well for any length of material—articles, essays, or full-length books.

Read the following examples of one-line hooks and the analysis that follows:

> In and through community lies the salvation of the world. (*The Different Drum: Community Making and Peace*, by M. Scott Peck, M.D.)

Analysis: This one-line hook introduces the subject of Peck's book and proclaims his position on the subject with the forceful words: "lies the salvation of the world." Purpose: to persuade. Audience: thoughtful adults of both genders who are probably socially responsible. Difference made: to convince people to build healthy communities. Promise: the author's deepest yearning—to foster peace. Emotional reaction: because of his selection of the word "salvation," I think he evokes a sense of urgency and perhaps even fear.

Here is an entirely different one-line hook:

> I am NOT going to whine. Yes, I have turned 50. (*Dave Barry Turns 50*)

Analysis: This master humorist begins his book with eleven words that do so much work! The emphasis on the word "not" tells us to expect the opposite, a lot of funny whining. We know that Dave Barry intends to entertain us, but if we did not know the author of this hook, I think we would still smile. His writing carries his purpose.

Difference made: besides giving us some laughs, I think this book offers to help baby boomers lighten up about their fears of aging. Audience: middle-aged and older. Promise: to give us courage by letting us know we are not alone. Emotional reaction: anticipation of having a good time.

QUESTION

The question lead is the easiest lead to write and is therefore the easiest lead to abuse. Rhetorical questions, questions for which an answer is obvious, are the worst. "Would you like to win the lottery?" Rhetorical questions are manipulative and can backfire by antagonizing the reader who feels used. With thought, an evocative question lead can start a piece just right.

> Rhetorical questions can backfire by antagonizing the reader who may feel manipulated.

> Nothing to fear but fear itself? Like most women, I understand the philosophical concept but less how to send fear running to its damp, dark closet. And I know I am not alone in this. At some

forever-to-be-remembered point in the lives of all women, they will lock arms with fear and dance a deadly tango. . . . And it will not be a matter of strength or weakness who is victorious, but who in its grip surrenders fastest, and in that moment of surrender glimpses the barest fragment of the thing fear fears most—faith. (Foreword by Lorian Hemmingway in *Femme d'Adventure: Travel Tales from Inner Montana to Outer Mongolia*, by Jessica Maxwell)

Analysis: Purpose: to entertain and inspire. Reader: women, probably ages thirty and up. Difference made: to get women to become adventurous, take risks. Promise: vicarious entertainment and the feeling of courage. Emotional reaction: identification with author. Eagerness to begin the journey with her.

Because of its brevity, the question lead can be ideal for fillers or other short articles.

Want the best workout plan ever? . . . Men who have sexual intercourse two or more times a week are fifty percent less likely to die from coronary heart disease than those who have sex less than once a month, according to research from University of Bristol in England and the Queen's University of Belfast. (*Reader's Digest*)

Analysis: Purpose: to inform and entertain. Reader: adult men and women. Difference made: hmm! To have sex at least twice a week! Promise: health and longevity. Emotional reaction: enjoyment. Surprise.

QUOTATION

A perennial favorite as a lead, a quotation should speak directly to the subject and slant of your article or essay.

Mark Twain wrote, "As to the Adjective: when in doubt, strike it out." Whether or not one takes this literally, his underlying message is: "Why use a word if it doesn't contribute to the clarity or beauty or strength of a sentence?" (*The Writer's Path: A Workbook*

to Release Your Creative Flow, by Todd Walton and Mindy Too-
may)

Analysis: Purpose: to instruct. Reader: writers and English students.
Difference made: to improve writing. Promise: competence. Emotional reaction: enjoyment of the Twain quote.

CONTROVERSIAL

When a writer wants to make her reader become as concerned as
she is, the controversial lead, also referred to as a "startling statement," may be the perfect one to begin the piece.

> Set your mood-altering goggles on "paranoia" and imagine the
> shopping mall of the future. From the moment you park your car,
> microscopic hidden cameras track your every footstep and casual
> glance. Inside, sensors on the merchandise record the color and
> style of each shirt you try on and note which magazines you
> browse and return to the rack. Central databases then gather and
> disseminate all of this information so that the next time you visit
> the mall, salespeople can scurry just ahead of you, placing items
> that you might like where you will be sure to see them. (*Fortune
> Technology Guide,* Winter 2001)

Analysis: Purpose: to persuade. Reader: men more than women,
probably eighteen to forty years old. Difference made: to stimulate
consumer action against invasion of privacy. Promise: to protect.
Emotional reaction: concern.

STATISTICAL

The use of statistics can pull the reader into an article or book,
especially if the numbers reveal something unexpected. The following statistical lead does just that:

> As everyone knows, the number of old people in the world is
> increasing rapidly. In the United States, there are now 33 million

men and women over the age of 65. In 1900, there were only 3 million. At the turn of the century, one could expect to live on the average only 47 years; today the figure is 73 for men and 79 for women. Between 1960 and 1994, according to the U.S. Census Bureau, the number of people over 85 rose 274 percent. Only 5 percent of those over 65 now live in nursing homes, and only 15 percent live with, and possibly receive care from, their families. Eighty percent, therefore, are living independently—either alone or with another person—and of those, 82 percent are said to be in moderate to good health. These gains are due to advances in medicine and the increased availability of medical services and to an improved standard of living. (*Enjoy Old Age: A Practical Guide,* by B. F. Skinner and M. E. Vaughan)

Analysis: Purpose: to inform. Reader: college-educated over fifty. Difference made: to bring a new perspective on aging. Promise: hope. Encouragement. Emotional reaction: relief.

SUMMARY

The summary lead is a version of "tell 'em what you're going to tell 'em." A lackluster lead in the wrong hands, it can be as compelling as any other lead. It offers a great way to preview information. Here is an example of a summary lead followed by an analysis of it:

Some people go caving for the sheer adventure of it—others, like me, go with hopes of finding treasure. On Mona Island, you've got a wide choice of loot to hunt for: Blackbeard's, William Kidd's, Jean Laffite's. Or perhaps you'd prefer the gold doubloons of Roberto Confresí. Or the strongbox of El Portugués, who legend has it, also buried the bodies of two murdered women on Mona. ("Hidden Treasure: Caving on Mona Island," by Bucky McMahon [*Islands,* July/August 2000])

Analysis: Purpose: to inform and entertain. Reader: anyone interested in adventure—armchair or actually going caving on Mona

Island. Difference made: to convince readers that they could hunt for, perhaps find, famous lost treasures. Promise: tantalizing adventure. Emotional reaction: excitement.

THEMATIC

You may wish to open your article or essay with a statement of your theme. The hook of a thematic lead is based upon the reader's interest in some universal issue of human need or of human character as developed in the writing. A thematic lead works particularly well for personal-experience essays and for memoirs.

> If ever there was a case that illustrates the mess of the health-care system in this country, it is *Rush Prudential HMO v. Moran,* now pending before the U.S. Supreme Court. Not that the Court can straighten out the nation's health-care plight by its ruling in this case, but *Rush Prudential* demonstrates how badly the health-care system can derail. ("Power Over Medical Decisions," by David C. Slade in *The World & I*)

Analysis: Purpose: to persuade. Reader: thoughtful adults. Difference made: to stimulate citizen participation. Promise: change. Emotional reaction: frustration with health-care system.

Choosing the Best Lead

With so many possibilities, how do you choose the best lead? As you learn more about the type of writing you wish to do—informative articles, personal essays, how-to books—you'll begin to see which leads *don't* fit. After eliminating these, one of the best gifts you can give yourself is permission to experiment. Don't limit yourself. Try writing all fifteen leads. Often, the third or fifth or seventh selection produces the writing that leaps off the page.

Map 5-2 provides a summary of the fifteen types of leads and the subcategories as well.

The Rest of the Beginning

In a filler or short article, the one-line hook can be the entire beginning. In many of the examples above, I cut the lead off after a sentence or two because the "lead" was finished. The lead is merely the hook; it must be followed by development and transition into the body of the piece.

More information about developing the beginning of your nonfiction piece will be covered in chapters eight through eleven. Basically, development takes the form of additional anecdotes, more facts and statistics, or leading the reader further into the details of your experience.

TRANSITIONS

Yet another part of the beginning of any piece of writing is the transition into the body. No one likes a bumpy ride. Transitions produce smooth reading and contribute to a piece's cohesiveness. If you begin with an anecdotal lead, for instance, your transition must be a clear statement of your subject or theme. Transitions bring the reader from your lead into the rest of your piece.

In terms of technique, a single word or phrase may signal a transition. This transition is the easiest—perhaps not the least visible—way to shift gears. Words such as "however," "so," "in addition," and "yet" are a few such transition words. Map 5-1 offers a longer list of transition words and phrases and their functions.

A typical transition from one sentence and paragraph to another is the introductory independent or dependent clause. An "independent clause," to review grammar, can "stand on its own." It is "independent" because it contains a subject, verb, and object. The independent clause in the following sentence is italicized: *"Although he had been to Boston as a child, [he was unprepared for the changes he saw.]"* A "dependent clause" does not contain all of the parts of a sentence and is thus "dependent" upon the rest of the sentence to be grammatically complete, such as *"In the 1900s,* everyone knew how to bake a pie."

A second kind of transition involves repetition of a word, phrase, idea, mood, or rhythm from a prior sentence or paragraph. Here is an example of word repetition based on an essay I wrote about my experiences on September 11, 2001, beginning with the last sentence of one paragraph and the first sentence of the next:

> The terminal had been evacuated, he said, because O'Hare was considered a possible target.
> *Target.* As his words sunk in, I stood dumbly in a line, twenty people in front of me, all of us waiting for answers from United Airlines' customer service, answers they couldn't give.

Yet another technique called echoing, or mirroring, is more subtle than prior ones. This form of transition echoes a concept or idea from the prior paragraph. Take, for example, an article on wildflowers that included a quotation from a homeowner who told the writer that deer had devoured all of her roses. The rest of the paragraph described how this led the homeowner and her husband to plant herbs and wild plants. Here are two echoing sentences, the one in a paragraph and the one of the next paragraph:

> So it was by default that nature was given its head at Willow Cottage—producing a spring scene that the owners sum up as "just smashing."
> The deer still come. ("Wild Flowering," by Tovah Martin in *Victoria*)

While you will need to make a transition between each of the three parts of any nonfiction piece, knowing how to make effective transitions is a technique to add to your toolkit for any kind of writing.

Ready to Begin Writing?

Not yet—except to practice writing leads. You have more planning ahead before raising the sails. When learning how to write nonfiction, each of these prewriting steps seems agonizingly slow. However, you'll soon see that your material makes decisions for you, and you'll eliminate most of the options in the lists. A good way to make use of the lists is to keep them handy to refresh your memory and to keep all options open.

MAP 5-1

Words and Phrases as Transitions

Transitions	Function
similarly, likewise, in the same way	Similarity
and, in addition, furthermore, also	Addition
first, second, third, again, so	Continuation
for example, for instance, in particular	Exemplify; Illustrate
in other words, specifically, that is, but, however, on the other hand, yet, still	Contrast
therefore, thus, then, consequently, as a result	Conclusion—result
in conclusion, finally, in summary, in short	Conclusion—summary
although, though, even so, granted that, even though	Concession
even this, indeed, of course	Emphasis

MAP 5-2

Review: Fifteen Types of Leads

1. Analogy or Comparison

2. Anecdotal or Case History

3. Combination

4. Direct Address

5. Factual

6. Journalistic

7. Metaphor

8. Descriptive or Narrative

9. One-Line Hook

10. Question

11. Quotation

12. Controversial

13. Statistical

14. Summary

15. Thematic

SIX

How Do I Develop the Middle?

Midway along the journey of our life, I woke to find myself in a dark wood, for I had wandered off from the straight path.

Dante Alighieri

WHEN YOU KNOW your subject, know what you want to say, and have a working title and lead that reflect a slant and promise, you're more than Aristotle's "well begun." Yet, more preparation lies ahead to create the most effective piece of writing possible.

The middle of any piece of writing fulfills the promise, the tease, of the beginning. The body of a manuscript fully develops your subject. Here is where the "rubber meets the road" or, extending the metaphor, where you could have a blowout or run out of gas if you don't plan ahead. In my editing business, one of the most common weaknesses I see in the middle of writers' work is disorganization—of sentences, paragraphs, and sections. These components may appear in the wrong order, or they may not belong in the piece at all. You can prevent these muddles of the middle by resisting the urge to write until you've created an outline of your work.

Before I introduce specific outlines for various types of nonfiction writing, I'd like to address a myth about outlining that is perpetuated by new and established writers alike. The myth goes like this: authentic writing—heartfelt, passionate, and artistic—cannot spring from an outline. Outlining excludes possibilities, limits creativity, and forces expression into a box.

> The right form eases communication and, in fact, becomes invisible to the reader.

"Get real!" I say. I believe that finding the best form for our literary expressions facilitates the expression itself. The right form eases communication and, in fact, becomes invisible to the reader. Like most artists, we writers must learn all about form and structure until their use becomes second nature. Only when we have mastered the techniques of writing well—including outlining and organizing—can we transcend those tasks—and then . . . only some of the time. In my experience, most writers who mount a defense against outlining don't hold such idealistic principles. Instead, they're merely avoiding one of the less enjoyable tasks we have to do. I don't blame them; I've avoided it, too.

Outlining does not necessarily mean reverting to the Roman numeral system you learned as far back as high school, or even elementary school. The starting point for developing a piece begins with selection of a method of organization that sets up the larger framework for a successful outline. This choice of organization of the whole work determines how to outline the line-by-line writing.

For instance, you may want to write about a personal experience. Your purpose is to inspire, the difference you wish to make is to save lives, your promise is to offer hope, and your slant is adrenaline—you want your reader to be afraid and take action. Your working title is "The Suicide That Never Should Have Happened." Your subject? The suicide death of your cousin. A heavy subject indeed.

You might assume that you should recite the events that led up to your cousin's death, one event after another as they actually happened. But that isn't the only way to organize such an essay, and it may not be the best way to organize it. You could, for instance, organize it as a story, which is very different than recounting it.

Like every other aspect of nonfiction writing, writers before you have cleared the brush and worn a clear path. I've identified eleven methods of organization, what some teachers also refer to as "ordering principles." Over the years, I have become the Mario Andretti of outlining and of writing fast because I save time and anguish by determining my method of organization first. Time spent planning is time saved writing.

Methods of Organization

The eleven methods of organization are:

- Analysis
- Analogy
- Cause/Effect
- Chronological
- Classification and division
- Comparison and contrast
- Inductive or deductive
- Order of importance or complexity
- Problem/Solution
- Sequential
- Story

ANALYSIS

This method of organization is the best choice when you wish to examine a subject in detail, and it often includes several methods of organization. Organization by analysis is a methodical, orderly process—the writer sorts the research material into logical divisions, and then divides these divisions into component parts. The parts then become the major headings in your piece. This method is well suited to technical material or a technical approach to any subject.

The Hero with an African Face: Mythic Wisdom of Traditional Africa, by Clyde Ford, offers an example of analysis as a method of organization. In one chapter, he introduces a heading, "The Quest for the African Hero," then explains that it involves three movements—the departure, fulfillment, and return. These are the "component parts" of the larger division of this chapter, introducing the reader to mythology and how it manifests in African cultures. Having named the component parts (the three movements of the journey), Ford introduces a Zulu myth and retells it in sections, offering analysis after each segment of the quest story. Every chapter of Ford's book uses analysis as the method of organization—following the same pattern of introducing concepts then illustrating them with stories and myths that are interrupted for analysis, explanation, and interpretation.

ANALOGY

We've seen that analogy can be used as a lead for any article, essay, or book. It can also be the primary method of organization for an entire piece, no matter its length. My friend the late Gaines Smith described analogy as most useful to "explain something unfamiliar in terms of something familiar, something unknown in terms of something known, and something remote in terms of something immediate." You may also wish to use analogy to explain something simple and then relate it to something more difficult, or vise versa. Analogy is a comparison, but its purpose is to draw similarities rather than differences.

Imagine the task faced by Daniel Goleman, the author of *Emotional Intelligence*. He knew the public was familiar with IQ, intelligence quotient. Nearly everyone has some idea about what emotional maturity means as well, but what is "emotional intelligence"? Goleman had coined a new description and faced the task of writing a book to explain it. Throughout the book, beginning with the title itself, he relies on analogy—and analysis—to organize his material. Early on he offers the idea of "emotional hijacking" to explain the more complex concept of how moments of explosive emotion—"good" and "bad"—cause a neural shift, turning the control of our actions over to the amygdala instead of the neocortex. Then he uses

> Analogy is a comparison, but its purpose is to draw similarities.

the analogy of a "tripwire" to describe the amygdala as it scans all experiences to determine whether it should take over. Analogy after analogy, all in service to helping the reader understand unfamiliar and complicated workings of the brain.

CAUSE/EFFECT

This method of organization can be used in either order—cause, then effect or effect, then cause. Astrology articles and books frequently organize their material by cause and effect. "Your Relationship Connection," by Diane Davis in *American Astrology*, describes the effect of the planet Venus when it is located in each of the twelve "houses" of a birth chart. Find your Venus in your lover's seventh house and the effect, she claims, could be marriage. Find it in your lover's sixth house, and you could be coworkers.

The cause-and-effect organization is best to use when you believe you have a strong case—evidence and support—for the causal relationship. This method is not preferable for relationships that involve a multiplicity of causes—or effects from one cause. Let's suppose that a high percentage of children from the same school are falling ill. What is the cause? Sick-building syndrome? A change in water quality? A bacteria in the cafeteria lunches? The power of suggestion? In other words, this method of organization needs to be selected with certainty about the direct relationship between the items you link together.

CHRONOLOGICAL

Putting your material in order by the march of time is an easy method of organization. Technically, chronological is a "sequential" method of organization, but it is so common that I have given it emphasis on its own. Most personal-experience stories are written chronologically. Even if a writer uses a different overall method of organization such as story order, substantial portions of an essay or memoir will be chronological.

The Perfect Storm, by Sebastian Junger, for instance, begins by introducing the reader to Bobby Shatford, the protagonist, Christina Cotter, his girlfriend, and the other people in this fishing village. The story continues in the order of the events of their lives, for the most part, leading up to the tragic and unbelievable storm. Nearly all autobiographies begin with childhood and continue chronologically through the author's life to the present day. Biographies, too, often follow a chronological order ending with the subject's death.

Because you need to hook your reader's attention, the beginning of an event may not be the most interesting place to start, or the clearest. That's why many stories begin with a time in the future or a time in the past and then jump to the beginning of the chronology for the main subject and event. Timothy Egan's literary true-crime book, *Breaking Blue,* hooks the reader and sets the context for the investigation by introducing a retired and ill police chief near the end of his life. The year is 1989 and Bill Parsons decides to "break blue" and tell the secret he has carried for thirty-five years. This lead defines part one. Egan begins part two in 1935, jumps to 1989 in part three, and finishes his "Epilogue" in 1990.

CLASSIFICATION AND DIVISION

You'll probably recognize this method of organization from high-school or college biology. First, you define a whole group, such as dogs. Then, you divide this whole into the "classes" that comprise it; in this case, working dogs, hunting dogs, etc. As you can see, each of these classes can be further classified into particular breeds of working dogs and particular breeds of hunting dogs.

Other than formal scientific classification and division, there are other kinds of writing for which classification and division is the best method of organization. For instance, take any of the things of a home—quilts, window coverings, chairs, tables, whatever—and you have a "whole" that you can divide into "classes." Classification and division is also an ideal method of organization for what is called the "roundup" article. These articles survey a whole group, such as hotels in New Orleans. The writer may then divide them into the classes of budget, economy, and luxury.

You may be wondering how classification and division differs from "analysis" as a method of organization. Classification and division *is* one of the tools of analysis, which encompasses many tools, such as definition of terms, explanation of complexities, and ordering by many of the organizational methods included in the list.

COMPARISON AND CONTRAST

This method of organization divides your material into two headings—similarities and differences. A common expression of this method is pro and con. Your job is to compare and contrast. Remember analogy? Analogy also relies on comparison via similarity, whereas this method offers the similarities and the differences.

For instance, the fun book *Do Not Talk to, Touch, Marry, or Otherwise Fiddle with Frogs,* by Nailah Shami, was given to me by a friend—for reasons I cannot fathom. While the book relies on the metaphor of the frog as the undesirable man, frogs and princes are contrasted throughout the book as the overall method of organization. Within each chapter, the author relies primarily on sequential order (see below). Croak versus croon—without any comparison of similarities. The relentless contrast drives home the point—for any woman who has not been able to, on her own, escape the lily pond.

A good example to illustrate both comparison and contrast as the exclusive method of organization is the article "Will That be Check or Credit," by Nora Caley in *Home Business* magazine. She describes payment by credit card, check, and money order and offers the advantages and disadvantages (the pros and cons) of each.

INDUCTIVE OR DEDUCTIVE

Just about every opinion or commentary piece uses inductive or deductive reasoning as its method of organization. You present an "argument" anytime you write something with the intent to persuade a reader to your viewpoint. Inductive organization begins (after the lead) with observations supported by evidence that eventually lead to a conclusion that is the writer's position on the subject. Deductive organization begins with a clear statement of the writer's position and then offers observations supported by evidence to prove it.

Many magazines and newspapers include a commentary or opinion feature in each issue. If you feel passionate about a subject, decide whether you want to make your conclusion known up front (deductive) or to lead your reader down the garden path to your conclusion using the accumulation of points and evidence (inductive). The full development of the "argument" form will be covered in chapter nine.

ORDER OF IMPORTANCE OR COMPLEXITY

The method of organization for the core of this book proceeds from less complex to more complex. The information of one chapter builds on the preceding one. Many instructional books are organized from simple to complex. When my editing associates and I decided to form a company, we began with no knowledge about how to do so. We read many books including *How to Profit by Forming Your Own Limited Liability Company,* by Scott E. Friedman. Thankfully, he began with definitions and the simple features of an LLC and then developed its complexity. Within individual chapters, he used comparison and contrast more than any other ordering principle. This was ideal to sort out the difference between sole proprietorships, c and s corporations, and partnerships. The happy result is our business, Editing International, LLC.

A beautiful little book that is organized by importance begins with what is most rather than least important. The book is *The Four Agreements: A Toltec Wisdom Book,* by Don Miguel Ruiz. The three agreements that follow the first one are each important, but they are "less important" because they depend upon the first agreement as a foundation. To some degree, the book proceeds from a simple and all-important first agreement, "Be Impeccable with Your Word," and then adds ideas that stem from and are related to this first important idea.

With this method of organization, you can choose an order that ascends or descends in importance or complexity.

PROBLEM/SOLUTION

Articles and books about the invisible realms of emotions, relationships, and spirituality often use a problem/solution method of organization. For instance, I'm a junky for information on health and well-being. Many of these articles introduce a medical problem, explaining what it is and how many people suffer from it, and then give various treatments.

A "classic" example of this method of organization is found throughout the magazine *Natural Health*. For example, "How to Stop Headaches for Good," by Robert Ivker, D.O., and Todd Nelson, N.D., introduces headaches in all their permutations and degrees of suffering. Then, the reader is offered seven natural remedies that promise to relieve them.

Writers can organize any personal challenges of a physical, emotional, or spiritual nature in this simple form. An essay by Al D. Squitieri Sr., also in *Natural Health,* even featured a "sidebar box" with the heading "Problem, Obstacles, and Solution." The essay followed the same format; his lead described the problem, the body of the piece described the obstacles under the heading "The Losses," and the solution under the heading "The Prayer." His conclusion, "The Promise," ended his essay.

When it comes to organizing more down-to-earth problems such as getting the slugs in your garden to raise the white flag, building a grape arbor, or changing your car's oil, the next method may offer a better organizing fit.

SEQUENTIAL

One of the most common methods of organization is sequential, the top choice for step-by-step instructions. It is the best method of organization for nearly all how-to articles and books.

Sometimes, articles do not have an "order of need." In other words, one step or instruction does not need to occur before or after another. "List" articles or books offer a perfect example. Using a numbers slant, the list becomes the sequence. One example of this numbers/list structure is the book *Dare to Lose: 4 Simple Steps to a Better Body.* The steps—sensible eating, exercise, relaxation techniques, and weight-loss supplements—need not be implemented in any particular order.

Another example of sequential organization is alphabetical order. Consider the following example of a list article that uses a numbering and alphabetical sequence for organization: "50 Foods to Help You Look and Feel Great," by Dina Aronson, R.D., in *Natural Health*. She begins with number one, apples, and ends with number fifty, wheat germ; one to fifty, and from letter "a" to letter "w." Aren't zinnias edible?

STORY

One of the most dramatic, and therefore effective, methods of organization for personal experiences is story. Have you ever read an essay or memoir and thought it read like fiction? Story order uses short-story form. This means that the story opens *in media res,* in the middle of a crisis or moment of change. This inciting incident introduces the problem that is the focus of the essay or memoir. The writer reveals how she sought to overcome obstacles but ran into greater ones. Finally, in the climax of the story, she vanquishes the last and largest of these obstacles and resolves the problem. In the process, she learns something fundamental about herself and life, thus echoing the story promise, revealing a clear theme, and making a difference in the life of her readers.

Joseph Campbell's Hero's Journey presents writers of books, such as memoir, biography, and even autobiography with one of the best blueprints for story organization. (See chapter eight for details.)

A second technique for developing any story including the personal-experience essay or article, nostalgia or humor, and memoir is the scene. Scenes convey events taking place at a particular time and place. In a word, action. Dramatic action. Using scene structure insures that your writing contains the most dramatic suspense and therefore the greatest satisfaction to the reader. Map 6-1 supplies the outline for scene structure.

A Word About Research

Because this is a book about how to write, I won't address researching in depth. However, an aspect of readiness to write involves matching piles and files of research with a method of organization.

Years ago, Harley Bjelland, one of my writing students, shared his way of organizing research that simplifies decisions into yes or no. Author of *Writing Better Technical Articles,* Harley described a process he dubbed the "Precedent Sort." Assuming that your research notes are on paper, you would take one paragraph, page, or grouping and decide whether it comes first. If yes, you put it under the correct category, say under "problem" of the problem/solution method of organization, or you place it first in a chronology or first in a sequence, and so forth. If your answer is no, you put the item aside and take up the next item.

Suppose you find an item that goes before the one you designated as "first." You simply put the new item first and the former item becomes second. You continue through your stack making one decision at a time. Eventually, if you use this methodical approach, you'll have decided the order of your materials, at least for the major headings covered in this chapter. You never need to make more than one decision at a time. Just yes or no. Simple! Thank you, Harley!

MAP 6-1

Outline of Scene Structure

1. Choose an action, location, and time.

2. Choose one person—yourself or your subject—as the principal narrator of the scene.

3. Reveal a goal that exposes the emotional truth of the narrator.

4. Show action toward reaching the goal.

5. Show opposition, by others or by circumstances, that blocks reaching the goal.

6. Reveal the selection of an alternate strategy for reaching the goal.

7. Repeat steps four and five as desired.

8. Show the goal reached or the impossibility of reaching it.

9. End the scene with a surprise, twist, or disaster.

10. Reveal the new emotional truth of the narrator.

MAP 6-2

Eleven Methods of Organization

1. Analysis

2. Analogy

3. Cause/Effect

4. Chronological

5. Classification and division

6. Comparison and contrast

7. Inductive or deductive

8. Order of importance or complexity

9. Problem/Solution

10. Sequential

11. Story

SEVEN

How Can I End Well?

On a journey of a hundred miles,
ninety is but halfway.
                    Chinese proverb

WRITERS OFTEN OVERLOOK the end of a piece of writing, the conclusion. Perhaps it appears overly simple. Yet, how you end an article, essay, or book can actually determine the value or effectiveness of the entire piece. Will your readers feel optimistic about their ability to follow your instructions? Will they understand the deepest emotion of your essay? Will they finish with a grin on their faces? Your readers' reactions and what they remember depend on how well you end.

Five Types of Conclusions

Five of the most common types of conclusions are as follows:

- Summary
- Callback
- Thematic
- Encouraging
- Quotation

SUMMARY

The easiest conclusion to write and among the most popular, especially for information-based articles, the summary often lists an article's main topics as its conclusion. For instance, an article titled "Magic Bullets Fly Again," by Carol Ezzell in *Scientific American,* describes the history of monoclonal antibodies since their discovery in the 1980s. (*Monoclonal antibodies* are clones of large B lymphocytes that produce antibodies to fight cancer.) The article provides current and projected clinical trials, their uses and potential, and the political atmosphere that affects cloning research. Appropriately, the writer uses a summary conclusion for what has been a summarizing article: "Whether they come from cattle, goats, corn, or bioreactors, monoclonal antibodies are set to become a major part of 21st-century medicine."

CALLBACK

Also referred to as a "tieback" and described visually as a "bookend," the callback conclusion refers the reader to the beginning of a piece, often using similar or even the same words. Writers especially favor the callback for essays and frequently combine it with a thematic conclusion. Consider the following first line and then a callback conclusion in an article titled "The Mysteries of Berkeley," written by Michael Chabon for *Gourmet* magazine:

> *Beginning:* "Berkeley. Where passion is married to intelligence, you may find genius, neurosis, madness, or rapture."

> *Callback conclusion, where the writer has been discussing Berkeley's quirky small businesses:* "A business that would never thrive anywhere else, in a city that lives and dies on the passion and intelligence, the madness and rapture, of its citizens."

Next, read a callback example drawn from "So . . . Are You Two Together?", a personal essay by Pagan Kennedy in *Ms.* magazine about the inadequacy of words to name the relationship of two women friends, not lovers, who live and work together:

> *Beginning:* "Liz is explaining the situation to some guy in customer service. 'My roommate and I need to network our computers together,' she's saying, seated at the other desk in the office that we share. The word 'roommate' jumps out at me. It's an inadequate word, but it's all we have. . . ."

> *Callback conclusion:* "She laughs and shifts her eyes away, a bit embarrassed by her own generosity. 'I couldn't have my roommate going around in shabby gloves,' she says. She uses the word 'roommate.' But I know what she means."

THEMATIC

For personal-experience essays and memoirs, and also for arguments—opinions and commentaries—a thematic conclusion drives home the take-away meaning a writer wishes the reader to conclude. A thematic conclusion fulfills the promise of a piece of writing.

In the first of a three-part series The American Family, *Better Homes and Gardens* featured "Finding the Way Back Home," by writer John Riha. His conclusion relies on a quotation to deliver the thematic statement and is thus a combination conclusion. Notice how the title of this article and the lead evoke a promise, a yearning, and also allude to deeper meaning.

> *Beginning:* "If there are places that will break one's spirit—and mend it again stronger than ever—the Absaroka Range of southern Montana's Rocky Mountains is one of those places. Here, where cottonwoods and aspens rustle beside crystalline creeks and raw fists of granite thrust 11,000 feet into a flawless blue sky, the original American Dream—that mythic confluence of hope, hard work, and self-determination—seems close at hand. It was here that three families recently slipped back in time—surviving for five months as 1800s pioneers. Challenged by hardships, they would come to discover the dream rooted deep in their own families."

Conclusion: " 'Back in the twenty-first century,' says Gordon, 'families often don't have common goals and purposes. We get scattered—there are too many distractions. Here, we work alongside each other, and the kids love it. The end result isn't the goal; it's the journey that matters. You cooperate, chip in, put your arm around each other when things get tough. That's what makes a family.' "

A firm statement, or restatement, of the author's position makes a thematic conclusion to an opinion piece. The argument, including its premise, the supporting evidence, and other elements form the body of the piece. In her opinion piece "Ad Nauseum," published in *Ms.* Magazine, writer Lisa Miya-Jervis opens with a description of the problem and closes with a thematic statement of her position.

Beginning: "Bikini-clad cuties cavorting in tropical paradise: just fine. Bimbos stripping down to display their goods for discriminating ladies: no problem. Kissing, groping, and nipple licking of all kinds: bring it on! A woman discussing with her husband the use of a contraceptive spermicide: no way. That's the position Fox Broadcasting Company took in January when it refused to air an ad for the spermicide Encare on an episode of its latest gleefully sleazy—and guiltily compelling—reality show, *Temptation Island.*"

Conclusion: "These television execs' hypocritical judgments give credence to the possibility that as advertising becomes more intrusive, the media will, in effect, be monitoring our sexual choices and dictating the 'proper' behavior of families—and yes, we should certainly care about that."

ENCOURAGING

The encouraging conclusion aims to leave the reader uplifted or empowered. This conclusion is often used at the end of how-to articles and books and at the end of inspirational essays and books.

An example of this kind of pep-talk conclusion comes from "The Business of Big Time," an article by Cynthia Whitcomb in *Writer's Digest*: "The more you understand the movie industry, the easier the transition will be from sandlot dreamer to rookie slugger in the major leagues."

In her article "Five Ways to Make Winter Tomatoes Taste Like Summer," in *Cooking Light,* writer Joanne Weir had but three paragraphs before offering the "five ways." Guess what her three paragraphs offered? A lead, a body, and a conclusion. For her conclusion, she summarized and offered encouragement:

> Five simple techniques—marinating, roasting, oven drying, grilling, and braising—improve the mealy texture of winter tomatoes and concentrate the pallid flavor to bring the off-season veggies to life. And with some experimentation, you'll quickly learn how to match the right method to any recipe.

QUOTATION

Use of a quotation conclusion—either from the subject of a human-interest piece or from a famous person, living or deceased, can give class and closure to your article or essay. Freelance writer Joanna Smith Rakoff ended her profile of author Nick Montemarano in *Poets & Writers* by quoting her subject. Because the whole piece focused on the difficulty, and finally the success, of getting his first novel published, the quotation at the end appropriately reflects this focus.

> He certainly may sleep a little better, simply because his story will be out in the world. "I feel relief that this story is going to be shared," he says. "But my feelings are more about the book than they are about me, more about the story being told than about me being its author. Writing, for me, is a means of self-discovery, and the book has already done what it's going to do for me—it happened in the writing of it. The publication is just an external thing."

Licking the Envelope

Some conclusions may not fully fit one of the five types, yet they deliver the feeling of conclusion to the reader. No matter how you write the endings of your articles, essays, and books, strive to give the reader a finished feeling. I call this "licking the envelope." A good way to find those words is to reread your lead. As T. S. Eliot said, "In my beginning is my end." Beginnings contain the seeds for endings, and endings reveal their roots in beginnings.

In the following four conclusions drawn from different categories of writing, I've italicized the words and phrases that deliver that finished, "ta-da" feeling:

> For now, the key to his moving on is this: sitting in a stationary armchair that neither vibrates nor roars. *Tomorrow, his only* company will be sea gulls, *his only* competition a bowling match with Brooke. *For a guy who lives for speed, not moving can be a good place to be.* ("The Boom in Vroom," a feature on racecar driver Jeff Gordon, written by Lynn Rosellini for *Reader's Digest*)

And another:

> The early evidence still holds: although there are some real differences between Red and Blue America, there is no fundamental conflict. There may be cracks, but there is no chasm. *Rather, there is a common love for this nation—one nation in the end.* ("One Nation, Slightly Divisible," by David Brooks in *The Atlantic Monthly*)

The next:

> If we don't fix this system, it won't matter if you have insurance or not," adds Roneet Lev of the ACEP [American College of Emergency Physicians]. "It will fall apart—*for all of us.* ("The ER Crisis," by Carol Lynn Mithers in *Ladies' Home Journal*)

Last of all:

> Wearing these bracelets [memorializing women who have died because of U.S. legislation] helps us remember, and giving them to friends will raise friends and consciousness. *It's a beginning.* ("Our Sister's Keepers," by Gloria Steinem in *Ms.* magazine)

The lead, the body, and the conclusion—the structure of all nonfiction. Now you can organize your research into these three parts and prepare to outline your particular piece. While you may have selected one of the methods of organization described in chapter six, you can gain even more help from knowing the organization that is typical for each category of nonfiction.

MAP 7-1

Choices for Ending Well

1. *Summary.* Summarize or list the main points in the article or essay.

2. *Callback.* Refer to the lead of your piece, calling the reader back to the beginning and to the story promise.

3. *Thematic.* Give a clear statement of the meaning of the essay or article, the take-away message or theme.

4. *Encouraging.* End with a statement or paragraph that encourages the reader, offers a pep talk or an optimistic attitude.

5. *Quotation.* Conclude with a quotation or with quoted dialogue that sums up the heart of the piece.

6. *Ta-da.* Use "concluding" language that leaves the reader with emotional closure.

EIGHT

Writing About People

Great men are rarely isolated mountain peaks; they are summits of ranges.

Thomas Wentworth Higginson

I STILL REMEMBER reading my first biography. You would have found me with my fourth-grade class in the school library pulling a book off the shelf entitled *Elizabeth Blackwell: The First Woman Doctor.* An electrifying thrill zinged through my body. As I turned each page and read about her life, I *was* Elizabeth Blackwell. By reading this one book, I had been changed. I shared her struggle and her triumph. But more than that, I had a new thought: I could be a doctor. No one in my family had gone past high school, much less to college or medical school. Years later, I did consider becoming a doctor (I wanted to be a Jungian analyst). To this day, I wonder if reading that first biography played a part in my becoming a doctor—a book doctor!

Nothing fascinates some readers—and writers—more than people. One can write about them through profiles, biographies, features, interviews, and essays. The writer can address humanity's most embarrassing failures and greatest triumphs. For those of us who find no more engaging a subject than me, myself, and I, personal-experience essays, sketches, memoirs, and autobiographies offer outlets for self-exploration and self-expression.

In chapter Six, you read about the eleven most common methods of organizing research: analysis, analogy, cause/effect, chronological, classification and division, comparison and contrast, inductive or deductive, order of importance or complexity, problem/solution, sequential, and story. When you write about people—others or yourself—you're most likely to use chronology, problem/solution, story, or a combination of these three. Coupled with your understanding about slant and leads, you may feel ready to outline and write your material. Yet, when writing about people, there's a whole new set of tools available to you. In this chapter, we'll talk about how to organize particular types of articles and essays about people according to the following patterns:

- B-C-B-A
- Emotional truth
- Story
- Hero's Journey
- Braided
- Mixed
- Self-help

B-C-B-A

The letters in the B-C-B-A pattern represent time—present, past, present, and future. This pattern is particularly helpful for outlining a profile. Most profiles introduce a noteworthy person, usually someone near the apex of their careers or contributions in life. In other words, "up-and-coming" subjects sell more copies in natural magazines than "has-beens" or "just-beguns." After the lead, the writer explains who the person is and why he or she is worthy of a reader's interest. Generally, the reason the person is of interest now, in the present, is because of some newsworthy accomplishment. Because newspapers and magazines are the major outlets for profiles, timeliness is key. In fact, you may not be able to sell a profile unless you can demonstrate a "news peg" or "tie-in." The present time information corresponds to B in this pattern.

After you've impressed readers with why they should be interested in your subject, you can segue to C, the past. C represents the long-ago past when the subject began the road to accomplishments or experienced a moment of realization that set the course for his or her choices over time. Chances are, the events in the past will also include mention of significant mentors, family members, or others.

Next, advance the chronology of your subject's life, bringing the reader back to B, the present, and add development to your introduction. Where next? A—the near future. What projects, contributions, or dreams does your VIP hold for the future? For example, what work in the present will become of public interest in the future? B-C-B-A. Now let's plug it in and analyze a profile.

APPLYING THE B-C-B-A PATTERN

Home Business magazine boasts "work-from-home success stories" in each issue. In effect, these are short profiles about everyday people, and they supply positive publicity for the subjects and their businesses. I found "Jason Hartman: Harnessing Energy to Become the Brand of Choice," by Marcus P. Meleton Jr. in the April 2002 issue, and tested it for the B-C-B-A outline.

Lead: Introduces Jason Hartman in the present [B], first personally, as a high-energy, curious person, and then professionally, as a motivational speaker and author of one book based on becoming a "brand," with a second book on its way.

Body: Goes back to high school and recounts how Jason got started on his present career track [C], tracing his success to recognition at ages twenty-one and twenty-four as a top sales and marketing professional. The writer continues to bring his history forward chronologically, interspersing quotations from Jason to explain his achievements and to promote the promise and slant of his book.

When the chronology returns to the present [B], the writer develops the ideas that were in the lead—Jason's search for and love of business trends and "gadgets" that help him to gain "productivity, mobility, and speed."

Conclusion: The last paragraph begins, "So what's next for Jason?" Now we've advanced to A, the future for this young entrepreneur.

You can detect—and use—the B-C-B-A pattern easily in short profiles, but it holds true for more sophisticated and complex profiles as well. What's the difference between a profile and a feature about an interesting or significant person? The only difference is in the development; generally, the feature offers the fullest development.

Emotional Truth

The core of personal-experience essays, character sketches, slices of life, memoirs, other styles of narrative (such as the travelogue), and autobiography is the presentation of an emotional truth. While it may not seem as if this is an outlining "pattern" for creative nonfiction, writing "from the inside out" using the emotional truth as the guiding light becomes the best guideline.

All of us experience life through the filter of our perceptions and values. When you write about an event or a portion of your life, it's that honesty that gives meaning to the events and resonates as authentic with the reader. Otherwise, your writing suffers from superficiality and leaves the reader thinking, "Why should I care?"

The best writing about the self or another evokes, reflects, and explores this deep-felt truth, beginning with the lead and continuing through to the last word. My friend and colleague, Bill Johnson, author of *A Story Is a Promise*, calls the central idea of a story the "dramatic truth." When you succeed at communicating the "heart" of your story, you create drama, and when that feeling comes directly from your heart, the reader will respond to its authenticity as the narrator's truth.

Self-reflection and even self-analysis will help you discover the emotional truth of each experience you write about. The process will also help you learn what questions to ask yourself or a subject of a profile or feature. Ask questions like:

- What's this experience or period of my life really about?

- What is the strongest feeling I still have about it?

- What emotional truth do I want to share with my reader?

- What emotional resolution did I undergo by the end of the experience or period of my life?

If you are writing the kind of essay that probes the depth of your experience, then ask another set of questions to get at another, perhaps deeper, emotional truth:

- What is the ugly truth about this experience or period of my life?

- What embarrassing or intolerable emotions do I have about it?

- What secret feelings do I harbor in reaction to the experience?

- What unfinished feelings am I still working through?

You can also place all of these questions in past tense, if you believe you've completed your personal growth relative to the experiences you write about. In the rest of the patterns for writing about people, you'll see that knowing the emotional truth is an all-important part of structure. In Map 8-1 I've listed some outstanding memoirs, and in the resource box that follows here, I've listed craft books on writing about people.

Story

For some features, biographies, personal-experience essays, and memoirs, the method of organization called "story" heightens suspense more than the B-C-B-A pattern, although the two patterns resemble each other. Story pattern moves chronologically, but also dramatically, in this sequence:

WRITING ABOUT PEOPLE
FURTHER RESOURCES

Memoirs of the Soul: Writing Your Spiritual Autobiography by Nan Phifer

✓ *Creative Nonfiction: Researching and Crafting Stories of Real Life*
by Philip Gerard

✓ *The Art of Creative Nonfiction: Writing and Selling the Literature of Reality* by Lee Gutkind

Writing Dramatic Nonfiction by William Noble

Writing Articles from the Heart: How to Write & Sell Your Life Experiences by Marjorie Holmes

Writing Creative Nonfiction by Carolyn F. Forché and Philip Gerard

✓ *Writing for Your Life* by Deena Metzger

✓ *Writing the Memoir: From Truth to Art* by Judith Barrington

Biographers and the Art of Biography by Ulick O'Connor

✓ *Inventing the Truth: The Art and Craft of Memoir*
edited by William Zinsser

- a triggering event

- introduction of a problem, a challenge, and an emotional truth

- exploration of the problem and challenge

- details of the struggle, the process, and the progress

- climactic success, resolution, and realization

- summary of future plans, actions, or a legacy

A TRIGGERING EVENT

Also called the "inciting incident" and "call to adventure," a triggering event puts the reader *in media res*. This Latin phrase means "in the midst of things." Instead of beginning your feature or essay, for instance, with an introduction, the lead drops the reader into the middle of the narrative.

INTRODUCTION OF A PROBLEM, A CHALLENGE, AND AN EMOTIONAL TRUTH

The triggering event introduces a problem that demonstrates how an individual copes with, and overcomes, adversity. In stories about highly accomplished people, the triggering event introduces a challenge in the subject's life. In both cases, soon after the setup of the event, the writer reveals the subject or writer/narrator's emotional truth. The emotional truth will always reflect some universal human need or yearning. Fulfillment of this need or yearning translates into one's promise to the reader.

For instance, many personal-experience essays open in the middle of a dramatic event: a runaway train, a near-death experience in the ICU ward, or a divorce decree. Each triggering event introduces a problem. The writer's promise to readers is to resolve the problem *and* reveal how the person—the subject of the piece or the writer—fulfilled that need. The need might be for courage (runaway train), for family unity (ICU story), for forgiveness (divorce decree), or any of a variety of other deep emotional yearnings.

Many feature stories open in the middle of a different kind of dramatic event: a scientific discovery, a charity drive, or a career stepping-stone. In these stories, the triggering event introduces a challenge, an obstacle—or several—in the way of success. The writer promises to show the reader how the individual meets the challenge, overcomes the obstacles, and reaches the goal. Once again, it's not only important to reveal the triumph but also to reveal how the individual fulfilled his or her yearning and, in the process, learned something fundamental about self and life. For example, the subject or narrator's yearning might be for healing (scientific discovery), belonging (charity drive), or sharing (career step).

EXPLORATION OF THE PROBLEM AND CHALLENGE

In this part of the pattern, the writer provides much-needed background. Sometimes, background includes definitions of terms and explanations of technical or scientific material. The exploration details evolution of the problem or the beginning of the challenge. Because the emotional truth has its roots in the past, details from the past can explain the origins of the person's need.

For instance, a person's dedication to searching for a healing remedy may be triggered by an episode in which she needed healing. A person's yearning for courage may be triggered by an incident in which he lacked courage. Remembering that these features or essays are about *people,* the writer must continue to develop the reader's understanding of the person. That means describing events in the life of the person and not just the person in the context of the events.

DETAILS OF THE STRUGGLE, THE PROCESS, AND THE PROGRESS

Whether your story describes how you or your subject sought treatments for a serious disease or fought for recognition in your career, this step in the pattern requires details of your *process* and landmarks of your *progress.*

Comparable to the structure of fiction, details of the struggle should build dramatically. Even though the full array of fictional techniques—from using dialogue to structuring scenes—will build drama, you can also build suspense by showing how the obstacles and challenges become fiercer over time—assuming they did. This builds story tension, and the result is greater reader interest in the outcome.

CLIMACTIC SUCCESS, RESOLUTION, AND REALIZATION

Your subject's moment of success will only be experienced as climactic if you work to build a crescendo of struggle. This step in the story is the climax. It resolves the initial problem engendered by the triggering event. You can also increase the reader's vicarious feeling of triumph if you provide your subject's feelings; physical sensations; quoted statements, conversations, or thoughts; and actions within the story environment. Write about sights, sounds, smells, tastes, tactile sensations, weather and temperature if appropriate, as well as inner feelings, memories, associations, and interpretations.

Because every "people story" should focus on development of the individual, this step should also resolve an inner, or psychological, problem that was activated by the triggering event. In so doing, the subject or the writer/narrator should come to realize something fundamental about the self and life. That something gives the reader a message, a theme, to carry away from the reading.

For instance, the runaway train story could resolve the subject's lifelong struggle with cowardice. The scientific discovery story might resolve the scientist's lifelong desire to heal others (perhaps fueled by the loss of someone to the disease being studied).

SUMMARY OF FUTURE PLANS, ACTIONS, OR A LEGACY

In a short story or novel, a "denouement" follows the climax. Denouement means wrapping up of loose ends, and it includes a demonstration of how the hero or heroine has changed. In the story pattern for nonfiction, the corresponding device is the "summary." The plans made or actions taken reveal what he or she has learned from the experience. These plans or actions demonstrate fulfillment of a yearning and realization of a change.

When a feature or essay recounts a struggle with a problem shared by thousands of others, then the summary may direct the reader on how to take action or to check resources provided at the end by the writer. That way, the story does not exploit anyone's misfortune for a reader's vicarious experience; rather, the story becomes a demonstration of hope and a resource for others facing the same problem.

If you are writing a biography about someone whose life or contribution exists in the past, then you may summarize that person's legacy. Chances are the legacy was a big reason you chose to write about the individual in the first place. A summary regarding your subject's ongoing legacy makes a fitting and satisfying conclusion.

APPLYING THE STORY PATTERN IN A REAL-LIFE DRAMA

Reader's Digest is infamous for its stories of real-life drama. Most display the story pattern, and their writers draw upon fictional techniques to provide moment-by-moment reenactments of the dramatic events.

Here is an analysis of "The Come Back Kid," by Mark Patinkin in the March 2002 issue of *Reader's Digest*:

The triggering event: The story opens *in media res* with the subject, Andrew Bateson, age six, in bed with a temperature of 102 degrees and, twenty-four hours later, with spots on his chest and stomach.

Introduction of a problem and a promise: Now at the hospital, the attending physician diagnoses Andrew's problem as meningococcemia, a fatal blood infection. The writer introduces the story promise (the medical fight to save Andrew's life) and the emotional challenge (the physician's determination to save his life and Andrew's determination to live).

Exploration of the roots of the problem: The writer describes how the bacteria are transmitted as well as the horrific details of what happens inside Andrew's body as the bacteria take over. Having provided the reader with medical explanations, the writer offers dialogue between the doctor and Andrew's parents to dramatize the information and reveal what's at stake: Andrew's life.

Details of the struggle, the process, and the progress: In this section, the writer carries the narrative through time and uses summaries, conversation, and inner dialogue to reveal the details of Andrew's deterioration and the efforts to save him. Most of the recounted dialogue is between the doctor and the parents and concerns Andrew's poor chances of survival, or the dialogue is between Andrew and his parents and involves information about the procedures. The writer uses "skip jumps" to move ahead several weeks at a time. This keeps the story focused on the most dramatic encounters.

Climactic success and resolution: Andrew survives amputation of his necrosis-ridden legs, but the writer prolongs reader investment in the outcome by maintaining suspense over whether Andrew will have the determination to learn to walk on prostheses and resume his former activities. At a turning point in the middle, Andrew asks his mother if he'll be able to walk again, to which she answers, "Oh, yeah. I've heard stories of kids who've done all kinds of things." (Notice how this reiterates the emotional promise of determination.) The resolution only comes after the writer shows us how Andrew overcomes his fear of not being able to walk, ride a bike, or skate and, through determination, succeeds.

Summary of future plans, actions, and a legacy: The conclusion shifts to the doctor's point of view one year later as she watches Andrew "on in-line skates as he flies down the street." She reflects on her uncertainty of his survival and the impact of her lifesaving efforts (i.e. determination). In essence, the last line reinforces the legacy of medicine and the Hippocratic Oath: "She [Dr. Kleinman] looks at it [a picture of Andrew] often, to remind herself of why she does what she does."

APPLYING THE STORY PATTERN IN A FIRST-PERSON ESSAY

The story pattern seems easy to find and use in a simple, linear story like Andrew's fight for life. But does the story pattern work equally well for a sophisticated first-person essay? The answer is yes. It is not the *only* way to organize a first-person essay, but using such a pattern supplies the kind of dramatic suspense associated with fiction. If your goal is to create heightened suspense, fictional techniques correspond to this end. The story pattern may be less effective for first-person experiences involving ideas versus events.

In prior chapters, I've mentioned the essay "Lost," by John Hildebrand in the 2000 winter issue of *Audubon*. His essay recounts his adventure with a friend in the wilds of British Columbia and how getting lost helped him find himself once again. Here is my structural analysis of its story pattern. Notice the reversal of order of the first two steps, an order that corresponds well with a more introspective essay.

Introduction of a problem, a challenge, and a promise: Through the metaphoric lead about the "right road" and "the dark woods," the writer introduces his problem: he's fifty and feels lost in his life.

The triggering event: A friend invites the author to go to the wilds of British Columbia. This is a "call to adventure" in the Hero's Journey, a challenge the writer accepts with the conscious idea of making it a "pilgrimage" of finding his way—the story's promise.

Exploration of the roots of the problem and challenge: The first exploration of this step in the pattern is literal; the writer offers details of the environment and the setting. As the literary and metaphoric backdrop of the piece, Hildebrand tells a story of another trip to the Yukon, describing how he learned the biological triggers that salmon use to find their way back to their natal streams. In the present story, when he encounters a Tahltan fishery on the Stikine River, he decides to climb the trail to get an overview of the crew helping fish over a landslide with hand nets.

Details of the struggle, the process, and the progress: As the writer recounts his cross-country hike, providing minute details of the setting, he also reports his struggle to keep the fishing crew in sight. He ends up following a bear trail, fails to retrace his steps back, and realizes he is lost.

Climactic success and resolution: With full details of his panic, including his physical reactions, his thinking, and immediate actions, Hildebrand intersperses parallels to *Hansel and Gretel* and leads us to the climax. He finds the path back, literally and figuratively, once again providing details of setting, philosophy, and parallels to the Tahltan peoples who once lived in the region.

Summary of future plans, actions, and a legacy: In the denouement, Hildebrand waxes philosophical, as one would expect in a literary essay: "What better way to discover the right road than to lose it now and then." In a one-paragraph conclusion, appropriately short for anti-climactic material, the writer tells of his return to his room, sharing his adventure with his friend over a bottle of Irish whiskey, and calling his wife. Alluding to the future and the realization he claims from his experience, Hildebrand ends his essay: "The phone rang two thousand miles away, and I wondered how to tell my wife that I'd lost my way for a while but had somehow managed to find the right road."

Hero's Journey

One of the great legacies to writers from the late mythologist Joseph Campbell is his identification of a storytelling pattern he named the "Hero's Journey." Found in stories from all cultures and time periods, the Hero's Journey is an archetype for the quest story. In the last decade, much has been made of its applicability to writing novels and screenplays. However, it also provides a superior method of organizing memoirs, biographies, and other book-length narrative nonfiction.

In brief, the Hero's Journey has four parts: Separation, Descent, Initiation, and Return. Within those four parts, the story has distinct steps, twelve in all (although nuances can add more). To learn about the Hero's Journey in depth, read *The Writer's Journey: Mythic Structure for Writers,* by Christopher Vogler. In brief, here is an explanation of the twelve steps. I've substituted narrator and subject for hero and heroine to better convey the application of the Hero's Journey to nonfiction:

1. *The Ordinary World/Hero at Home.* Establishes the narrator/subject's ordinary life and sets the stage for contrast with the special world of the challenge.

2. *Call to Adventure/The Challenge.* Introduces an upsetting incident, a problem, and a challenge, and defines what's at stake—what could be lost or gained.

3. *Refusal of the Call/Elimination of Expendable People.* Reveals the narrator/subject's natural resistance to change and fears about what lies ahead. Sometimes shows how people close to the narrator/subject leave—through death or everyday circumstances.

4. *Wise Advisor/Acceptance of the Call.* Introduces a mentor who encourages the narrator/subject to overcome fear and resistance and accept the challenge—because he or she is the only one who can.

5. *Crossing the Threshold/The Special World.* Follows the narrator/subject into the "special world" of the problem and its resolution, a world in contrast to the ordinary life. Shows the "leap of faith" required to pursue the goal and resolve the problem.

6. *Road of Tests and Trials/Allies and Enemies.* The narrator/subject finds friends and encounters opposition by people or events. The difficulties force the narrator/subject to draw upon skills and hidden resources.

7. *Approaching the Inmost Cave/Belly of the Whale.* The narrator/subject gets to the crux of the problem, tries everything to resolve it, and appears to fail. Immobilized and disheartened, the narrator/subject all but gives up hope, and in doing so, faces his or her greatest fear and character weakness.

8. *Life and Death Struggle/Seizing the Sword.* Offers moment by moment details of the narrator/subject's final struggle to reach the goal, showing how she or he taps a character strength to vanquish opposition and succeed.

9. *Moment of Triumph/Refusal of the Return.* The narrator/subject celebrates success, expressing the full range of emotions, and doesn't want to deal with the past or contemplate the future.

10. *The Return.* The narrator/subject "faces reality," commits to finishing loose ends and returning home, home meaning to the self, loved ones, and sometimes the physical location where the journey began.

11. *The Ultimate Test/Resurrection and Rebirth.* Shows the narrator/subject being tested within and without to demonstrate character change, integration of the old self, which was dogged by a weakness and need, and the new self, which has greater awareness and self-acceptance.

12. *Master of Two Worlds/Return with the Boon or Treasure.* Having passed the final test of character growth and integration, the narrator/subject is a person reborn into a new self. With the reward of having reached the goal, of fulfillment of her or his yearning, the narrator/subject returns home to share this enhanced knowledge. In addition, there may be a physical manifestation of the reward.

One of the great organizational nightmares for anyone writing a memoir, autobiography, or biography is deciding what is important and meaningful and what is unimportant and extraneous. "Just because it happened doesn't mean it's interesting," goes the old saying. Because the Hero's Journey is a universal pattern that describes human responses to change and need, most writers find this pattern useful for selecting what is important.

Braided

For more complex pieces, the straightforward B-C-B-A pattern, the simple story pattern, or even the more complex Hero's Journey may not suit the material or the writer's vision. In the last decade, a new label—and the flowering of a distinct genre—has emerged for literary essays, biographies, nature writing, and memoirs. This new label is "creative nonfiction." The foundation of this writing is factual but the manner of writing is "creative."

Carolyn Forché and Philip Gerard, editors of *Writing Creative Nonfiction,* describe creative nonfiction as "storytelling of a very high order—through the revelation of character and the suspense of plot, the subtle braiding of themes, rhythms and resonance, memory and imaginative research, precise and original language, and a narrative stance that is intelligent, humble, questioning, distinctive, individual, and implicitly alert to the world."

The "braided" pattern means exactly what it describes; the writer develops and braids several "strands" of narrative. In some essays or memoirs, different people may constitute the different strands. In other works, distinct events, memories, or images define them. Organizationally, the writer relies on one theme to unify the separate strands and upon the "hiatus"—either four line spaces or a series of asterisks—to visually mark a change from one to another. Thus, you have the braiding pattern: strand, hiatus, strand, hiatus, and so forth. A simple example of the braided pattern is *The Color of Water,* by James McBride. The memoir moves between James, a black man, and his Jewish mother. A complex example of the braided pattern is *For the Time Being,* by Annie Dillard. Some of the strands include: scenes from a paleontologist's explorations in the deserts of China, contemplations about Hasidic Jews of Eastern Europe, a natural history of sand, individual clouds and their movements in time, birth defects in humans, encounters with strangers, narrative segments about modern China and Israel, and information about our generation. Other, simpler, perhaps clearer braided patterns can be found in *Fathers, Sons, and Brothers,* by Bret Lott, and *The Low Road: A Scottish Family Memoir,* by Valerie Miner. Lott's memoir is told by one voice that weaves the stories of three generations of men. Miner's memoir is, as she describes, "A concert of voices": her mother's in first-person past tense; the grandmother's in third-person past tense; the author's voice in first-person present tense; and her grandfather's in second-person poetic. Each chapter features one voice, and the chronology moves back and forth from 1865 to the present.

Mixed

If you are called to this "storytelling of a very high order," does that mean structure be damned? To the contrary, I recommend finding a pattern that comes closest to your needs and adapting it. Consider the mixing of patterns by author A. Scott Berg, one of our finest biographers. Although he has written acclaimed biographies of Samuel Goldwyn and Charles Lindbergh, I'm partial to his biography *Max Perkins: Editor of Genius,* about the legendary Scribners editor. Berg's seven-year effort (not counting the previous year's work on Perkins for his thesis) won Berg the National Book Award. Examining the book for its structural spine reveals his use of patterns we've covered.

In terms of time, the biography follows B-C-B-A. Beginning in March 1946 (B), Berg then moves the narrative back to 1919 (C) when Perkins made his first literary discovery. Berg "backfills" with a chapter about Perkins's childhood, parents, and school experience, the long-ago past and a context for the biography. The rest of the book continues chronologically to March 1946 (B) and then through Perkins's death and funeral in June 1946 (A).

Although the simple pattern fits the organization of this 451-page work, it would be insufficient for conveying the complexity of the story and for creating the level of reader involvement that Berg accomplishes. While I do not know if the author knew about or used Campbell's Hero's Journey as one of his outlining tools, the biography does include all twelve steps.

> "Biography is a very definite region bounded on the north by history, on the south by fiction, on the east by obituary, and on the west by tedium."
>
> **Philip Guedalla**

Berg also demonstrates the technique of braiding. Although Maxwell Perkins helped dozens of authors, the biography focuses on his personal and professional relationship with three: F. Scott Fitzgerald, Thomas Wolfe, and Ernest Hemingway. As Berg braids the three men's personal and literary lives into the main story, the reader gets to know these authors almost as well as they do Perkins, the subject of the biography.

Self-Help Pattern

Self-help books and articles are really about people, too; authors of self-help seek to help readers improve themselves and their relationships. When you write for a self-help audience, you must hold one thing constantly in mind: the reader's need. If a woman's marriage is on rocky ground, she will fervently hope to glean help from your article on how to save troubled marriages. If a father has just lost a son, he will cling to every word in an article about finding meaning in the death of a child. Stray from the readers' need and you risk antagonizing them or losing them altogether.

LEAD

As you'll remember, the first component of any piece of nonfiction is the lead. While any lead mentioned in chapter five will work, the anecdote or case history is by far the most common lead for self-help writing. You can create fictional people involved in fictional situations or use case-history examples altering the actual names. Sometimes real people and their real names will be used ... with permission, of course. The power of the anecdotal lead lies in featuring people—just like your reader—who struggle with a particular problem—identical to the readers' problem.

The rest of the organization of the body of self-help articles and essays follows this pattern:

- Problem
- Definition
- Solution #1
- Example

- Solution #2
- Example
- Solution #3
- Example and so forth

PROBLEM

After your lead, you must offer a clear statement of the focus of your article or book. That focus will be the problem for which you offer a solution or advice. All self-help writing promises the reader tools—knowledge, techniques, perspective—that enable readers to resolve their problems by themselves. The primary difference made by all self-help is relief from suffering and an increase in problem-solving skills.

DEFINITION

Your statement announcing the subject of your article or book should include or be followed by a definition of the terms that will be used in the piece. Many writers fail to define their terms, assuming that the reader will know what they mean. Be aware that even commonly used terms in the self-help vernacular such as desire, love, affection, resentment, hate, forgiveness, communication, and feelings carry highly individualized and emotionally charged meanings. If you use and fail to define common "psychobabble" terms such as "defense mechanism," "denial," "processing," "echoing," "self-esteem," or "owning," you risk losing your reader and coming off sounding like a self-important parrot.

SOLUTIONS

The key to writing effective self-help articles and books is to stick close to the problem/solution method of organization. If your solutions build one upon another, you may also need an overall framework of an ascending order of complexity.

EXAMPLES

Essential to effective self-help writing are examples to support, demonstrate, or explain nearly every point. If you consider that your reader is "living through" the people in your writing, you'll see how important it is to give them plenty of opportunities to relate to the human application of your ideas. Besides offering clear definitions of your terms, a vignette may communicate better than a thousand words. For example, everyone knows what an "echo" is but may still need a demonstration of the technique of "echoing":

> *Bob:* After taking care of the kids all day, doing laundry, and cleaning house, I'm desperate for adult conversation.

> *Kim:* Let me see if I understand you; after being alone all day with kids and chores, you really need to talk with an adult.

The most frequent mistakes I've seen as an editor of self-help manuscripts is too much theory, too much of the author's personal experience, academic diction, and too few examples.

EXAMPLE OF SELF-HELP PATTERN

Typical of articles in women's magazines, "Nail Your Next Interview" in *New Woman* addressed the problem of failing to get jobs from interviews. The staff writer introduced the guest authority, Anne Sweeney, president of the Disney Channel and the Disney/ABC Cable Network. The concept of "job interview" needed no definition. Instead, the article identified eight solutions. Each one was named in turn, followed by a quotation from Sweeney that contained an example or vignette of either the problem, the solution, or both. Here's an example of one of the paragraphs.

> *Skip the gossip.* "Never bring up rumors you may have heard about people in the industry. A candidate once told me, 'I know you're interviewing so-and-so, and I gotta tell you, she's not that great.'

That just told me that the guy in my office wasn't great, since he felt the need to bad-mouth the competition."

Problem-solution-example. This pattern works just as well for more complex material.

Putting It All Together

Now you've got all the tools you need to successfully map whatever "people story" you wish to write. In summary, you've selected your idea and gathered research. You've decided on one of the four purposes, and you've thought about how you want to make a difference in your readers' lives with this particular piece of writing. You have in mind what deep issue of human need will be reflected as an unfulfilled yearning by your narrator and as a promise to the reader.

Next, you chose a slant and a working title. You tried out different leads until you found the right entrée into your work. Looking over the list of methods of organization, you selected the one or several that best fit your project. You began to sort your research materials into piles or files that match this larger schematic of organization.

Last of all, you decided which pattern best facilitates the kind of people story you are writing; you've got the exact map for your specific piece. Finally, you decided which scene comes first, if appropriate, and outlined it. What's next?

Writing.

MAP 8-1

A Reading List of Outstanding Memoirs

ON BAD CHILDHOODS:
Fierce Attachments by Vivian Gornick
This Boy's Life by Tobias Wolff
✓ *A Hole in the World* by Richard Rhodes
The Bonesetter's Daughter by Amy Tan
Welcome to My Country by Lauren Slater
Angela's Ashes by Frank McCourt

ON HAPPY CHILDHOODS:
An American Childhood by Annie Dillard
✓ *Hunger of Memory* by Richard Rodriguez
Becoming a Man by Paul Monette
Uncle Tungsten by Oliver Sacks
The Best Thing I Ever Tasted by Sally Tisdale

GOING TO SCHOOLS:
Black Ice by Lorene Cary
Through the Narrow Gate by Karen Armstrong

ABOUT ILLNESS, DISABILITY, RECOVERY:
Borrowed Time by Paul Monette
It's Not About the Bike by Lance Armstrong
Mommie Dearest by Christina Crawford
Sybil by Flora Rhea Schreiber
✓ *Tuesdays with Morrie* by Mitch Albom
Still Me by Christopher Reeve

ON MARRIAGES—GOOD AND BAD:
The Hacienda by Lisa St. Aubin de Teran
I Closed My Eyes by Michele Weldon

COMING OF AGE, COMING OUT, AND INSIDE THE FAMILY:
✓ *Memories of a Catholic Girlhood* by Mary McCarthy
I Know Why the Caged Bird Sings by Maya Angelou

MAP 8-1

Continued

Annie John by Jamaica Kincaid
Minor Characters by Joyce Johnson
Restoring the Color of Roses by Barrie Jean Borich
Stone Butch Blues by Leslie Feinberg

OVERCOMING MENTAL ILLNESS:
Darkness Visible by William Styron
An Unquiet Mind by Kay Redfield Jamison
Nobody Nowhere by Donna Williams
The Magic Daughter by Jane Phillips
✓ *Traveling Mercies* by Ann Lamott

UNCERTAIN IDENTITY:
Broken Vessels by Andre Dubus

ON WAR:
In Pharaoh's Army by Tobias Wolff
American Daughter Gone to War by Winnie Smith
Dear Mom: A Sniper's Vietnam by Joseph Ward
See No Evil: The True Story of a Ground Soldier in the CIA's War on Terrorism by Robert Baer

CONFRONTING RACISM/SEXISM/FASCISM:
The Color of Water by James McBride
Nine Parts of Desire by Geraldine Brooks
✓ *Man's Search for Meaning* by Viktor Frankl
Anne Frank: The Diary of a Young Girl

ABOUT LIFE AND DEATH:
The Wheel of Life by Elisabeth Kubler-Ross, M.D.
Still Here by Ram Dass

MAP 8-2

Summary of the Hero's Journey Pattern

THE SEPARATION AND DEPARTURE
The Ordinary World/Hero at Home
Call to Adventure/The Challenge
Refusal of the Call/Elimination of Expendable People
Wise Advisor/Acceptance of the Call
Crossing the Threshold/The Special World

THE DESCENT AND INITIATION
Road of Tests and Trials/Allies and Enemies
Approaching the Inmost Cave/Belly of the Whale
Life and Death Struggle/Seizing the Sword
Moment of Triumph

THE RETURN AND RESURRECTION
Refusal of the Return
The Return
The Ultimate Test/Resurrection and Rebirth
Master of Two Worlds/Return with the Boon or Treasure

NINE

Writing About Ideas

A lie gets halfway around the world before the truth has a chance to get its pants on.

Sir Winston Churchill

I WAS A SOPHOMORE in high-school English class and, always a sucker for extra credit, I figured I'd pick up some "free" points and lock in my A. My teacher, the brilliant and charismatic Mel Weiser, had a different purpose; he'd designed his extra-credit projects to develop our minds. Cocky and confident, I remained after class and requested the assignment. He handed me a sheet of paper with one question typed on it, all the while watching my face.

"What is thinking?" I read aloud. A rising inner heat sent a line of sweat trickling down my rib cage. I always had trouble standing closer than three feet from Mr. Weiser, and now, closer than that, his intense stare permitted no escape.

"Yes," he said firmly. "Write an essay about what you think thinking is."

I don't remember the rest of our interchange, but I do remember my first encounter with the blank page and the limits of my mind. I'd read Descartes's postulate "I think; therefore I am." But that evening, I sat at our shiny, Formica kitchen table with a great *tabula rasa*—within and without.

I wish I had kept my essay and the next one, my last before I gave up on Mr. Weiser's *impossible* assignments, an essay on the question, "What is dreaming?"

Writing about ideas is not for the faint of heart or the shallow of mind. Ideas, abstract by definition, define our humanness. Writing about them allows us to explore the furthest

Writing about ideas is not for the faint of heart or the shallow of mind.

reaches of what it means to be thinking and feeling individuals.

Three broad categories help define the whole arena of ideas:

1. Big Ideas. Philosophy, metaphysics, religion, and science all deal with Big Ideas: What is the nature of life? What is existence? Who am I? Why am I? What is the meaning of life? The easy questions for which not a soul on earth has "the" answer.

2. Important ideas. Important ideas contribute to defining the Big Ideas. They cover every discipline, subject area, and concern: love, hate, faith, trust, courage, loss, betrayal, friendship, and family, and abstractions such as aesthetics, morality, and human rights.

3. Ideas that inform us about the world around us.

Some ideas focus on things—the visible world, natural and man-made, rather than the invisible and intangible world. These ideas might include cell division, backpacking trails in the Rockies, or child-rearing methods. Some writing about ideas involves information for its own sake or explores the idea makers, i.e. people.

The structure for writing about things, information, and people, relative to ideas, is covered in chapters eight, ten, and eleven. This chapter covers how to write about ideas—big, important, and simply close to your heart—when your desire is to convince readers to agree with you.

Defining the Study of Ideas

Guidelines for how to write about big and important ideas lead us back to Plato and Aristotle in the Indo-European tradition and to

Lao-tzu and Confucius in Asian traditions. Every continent and culture offers authorities and scholars who define, for that culture, how to talk and write about ideas. Most writing about ideas in English-speaking publications rests on methods of logical inquiry developed in Western philosophy. Before I introduce the main patterns for writing about ideas, some basic definitions are in order, according to Webster:

> *Philosophy:* "A study of the processes governing thought and conduct; theory or investigation of the principles or laws that regulate the universe and underlie all knowledge and reality; included in the study are aesthetics, ethics, logic, metaphysics, etc."

These areas of study inspire most of the essays published in magazines, journals, and books. Here, too, are definitions of aesthetics, ethics, metaphysics, and logic:

> *Aesthetics:* "The theory of the fine arts and of people's responses to them; the doctrines of taste."

> *Ethics:* "The study of standards of conduct and moral judgment; the system or code of morals of a particular philosopher, religion, group, profession, etc."

> *Metaphysics:* "The branch of philosophy that deals with first principles and seeks to explain the nature of being or reality (*ontology*) and of the origin and structure of the world (*cosmology*); it is closely associated with a theory of knowledge (*epistemology*)."

> *Logic:* "The science of correct reasoning; the science which deals with the criteria of valid thought. Necessary connection or outcome, as through the working of cause and effect."

Even if you only want to write a letter to the editor of your newspaper, knowing whether your Big Ideas, Important Ideas, or Informational Ideas are based in philosophy, aesthetics, ethics, or metaphysics can greatly enhance the effectiveness of your writing.

One doesn't have to be writing about something lofty. Even if you write about an everyday matter, applying these structural ideas will improve your writing. Let's use the example of one of my pet peeves. As an extra-tall frequent flyer, I wince when my "lowest fare" seat compresses my body into a space that would give pause to a Chinese acrobat. As a problem solver and idealist, I've considered the situation and have arrived at *the* solution! All of the first-class seating should be torn out and the added space equally apportioned to all of the seats. Even more progressive (if I were in charge), I'd have a block of seats custom-made for people with special needs. I'd create a row or two of seats accommodating individuals over a certain weight. Another few rows would have extra legroom for those of us who are over six feet tall (or over a certain leg length). My ideal airline would also have custom seats for parents with children and babies.

What kind of essay is this? We can safely rule out philosophy, aesthetics, and metaphysics. I'm not arguing reality, beauty, or religion. On the surface, I'm arguing for comfort, but the deeper issue illustrated by my approach to this subject is ethics—an issue of moral conduct. In other words, the present design and availability of airline seating is based on money and class. My essay would argue that airline seat design and availability should accommodate the individual's need, independent of social class or ability to pay.

Should my approach in writing be based in logic or in emotion? Either is a legitimate, but one may be more effective than the other. Knowing that my essay has roots in ethics helps me choose how to develop from the various methods of persuasion.

Methods of Persuasion

Your intent, whether explicitly stated or not, is to influence readers along the lines of your thinking. Once you select an idea and determine that it has roots in philosophy, aesthetics, ethics, or metaphysics, you can decide whether to use logic or emotions to persuade people to adopt your views.

If one selects a logical approach, then the method of organization should be inductive or deductive reasoning. Or, if the argument will be stronger, one might select cause-and-effect reasoning.

For years, I've kept inductive and deductive reasoning clear in my mind by thinking of inductive reasoning as the "sneak attack" and deductive thinking as "the falling piano." Inductive seems sneaky because bit by bit the writer offers evidence until the accumulated pile points to an obvious conclusion, which just happens to be the opinion the writer wants you to reach. You won't find the inductive argument in exceedingly short pieces, because the writer needs room to introduce point after point, evidence after evidence. Rachel Carson's *Silent Spring* offers the inductive approach. Credited with creating an awakening of the American ecological and environmental consciousness, Carson took the reader into one after another life form. She showed us the fragility of life when exposed to man-made hazards, especially toxins. The conclusion by book's end, for a generation of her readers, was that human beings are harming the environment, upsetting the natural balance, and we must stop.

Deductive reasoning reminds me of a falling piano because the writer makes his or her opinion known at the beginning of the writing, and all of the points and evidence serves to support that opinion. The reader is never in the dark. It's as if the reader is on the fifth floor of a building when the piano tumbles out a very large window. "Yup, it's a piano," we say, "and there it goes." No question, we know where it's headed, and gravity confirms its inevitable splatter on the sidewalk below. The beautiful, enormously influential little book *Small Is Beautiful: A Study of Economics as if People Mattered,* by Ernst Schumacher, makes an impassioned plea for appropriate technology, "technology with a human face," which from title to last word is as clear as . . . a falling piano.

In our times of technological and even scientific sophistication, the public is very accustomed to persuasion based on cause-and-effect reasoning. Pavlov's dog is a great example of this structure. The bell rings and the dog salivates. Cause. Effect. A complex, provocative, and important book that introduces many cause-effect arguments is *The Future of Life*. Author Edward O. Wilson, two-time Pulitzer prizewinner, describes that as America consumes (cause), and the rest of the world tries to keep up, biological diversity diminishes (effect). In turn, loss of biodiversity (cause) triggers economic losses to a number of industries (effect).

What if a writer prefers an emotional appeal over logical reasoning? How might I do this with my essay about airline seats? I could describe the suffering by actual people I interview and the consequences of being squished into seats too small for them. Research will unearth cases of people who have died of blood clots for lack of circulation in their legs. I could use complaints from obese travelers who literally could not fit in their purchased seat and had to pay for two seats, or use complaints from others who suffered discomfort from their overweight seatmates. How many incidents have there been of documented medical trauma directly related to airline seating? Readers identify with, and respond to, stories about suffering, and they don't need logic to reach an opinion. Politicians know this!

Whether your reason for writing about an idea is to solve problems, make decisions, or justify a position, your essay opens a dialogue with your readers.

Argument and Its Parts

The formal term for writing about ideas is "argument." Once you decide on the idea or position you want to convey, you should decide whether to make a logical, emotional, or ethical appeal to convince the reader.

Remember the methods of organization covered in chapter six? Look through the list at the end of that chapter and decide which methods might work best for your idea. Besides inductive or deductive reasoning, or cause and effect, classification and division might be useful. A story pattern may even work here. Parables, for instance, remain one of the most potent ways to present ideas and influence others.

Arguments have a number of specific parts, each of which involves making a decision that determines the effectiveness of your writing. These parts are audience, proposition, definitions, claim, support, and warrant.

AUDIENCE

One of the difficult aspects of writing a letter to the editor, or even a commentary piece, for a local newspaper is that the audience is so diverse. When you write about an idea, you should assess how much your audience already knows, whether they are divided or in agreement on the issues you raise, and how emotionally invested they are in the issues. Finding common ground is important at the beginning of an essay; your reader thus begins the piece agreeing with you to some degree.

PROPOSITION

The proposition is the answer to what you are trying to prove. It doesn't matter if you are presenting an idea about a religious belief, a political position, or a social concern. For your own clarity, organize your thinking by writing a one-line proposition. You can even start your sentence with "I propose," such as "I propose that elementary-school lunches are contributing to a host of childhood diseases, from diabetes to attention deficit disorder." A cruder version of this proposition, when published in an elementary-school newspaper that was carried home to parents, caused such alarm that the furious principal called the frightened editor into his office. How well I remember that dressing-down—and the power of the pen. When you begin to write your piece, no matter its length, you'll translate your proposition literally or figuratively into your lead.

DEFINITIONS

Defining terms is a critical part of communicating effectively. In an argument, defining your terms—or your interpretation of the terms—establishes a foundation of clarity and trust for your entire essay. One of the most common errors that writers, including my-self, make is to omit definitions. It is ever so easy to assume that your reader knows exactly what you are writing about. Doesn't everybody know stock futures, amortization, dividends, compound interest, and depreciation? No, they don't—so don't be afraid to overexplain.

CLAIM

Once you establish your proposition and have written your lead, you are ready to make a transition into the body of your argument. A good tactic is to concede a point to your opposition. For one, that shows your reasonableness. Second, your concession paves the way for your reader to concede—to you.

You'll make claims about your proposition as a way of offering proof. There are three kinds of claims: of fact, of value, and of policy. Claims of fact offer objectively verifiable data. Claims of value express approval or disapproval of taste or morality. They evaluate desirability. Movie reviews are a good example. Claims of policy suggest institutionalizing change as a solution to problems, such as "There ought to be a law."

SUPPORT

Your claim is one thing; you've probably heard a naysayer state, "You can claim anything." It's true; you can *claim* anything . . . but how do you prove it? Support describes what you use to bolster your claim and win the reader over to your proposition.

Here again, you have three very different choices for how you produce support: evidence, motivational appeal, and inference.

Evidence means "hard" facts, objective and verifiable: statistics, first-person testimony, and expert opinion.

Motivational appeal seeks reader support for the claim based on val-ues and attitudes. For instance, if I said that 100 percent recycling, return, and reuse is not only doable but should be legally mandated,

I could seek support by insisting that no species has the right to reduce the quality of habitat for any other species. This would be a motivational appeal based on a claim of values.

Inference uses interpretations of facts, sometimes as if they are facts, for support. Inference is "slippery." I associate it with faulty reasoning aimed at manipulation and being sneaky. Example: The number one priority for any politician is getting reelected. Senator John Doe's vote on Bill 10-10 proves he's thinking about the fall election.

WARRANT

Remember the "warranty" that came with your last purchase of an electronic item? Let's suppose that you were trying to make up your mind to buy one of two digital cameras. They are identical in every way. One, however, carries an endorsement from *Consumer Reports* that says it was number one in their 2002 test of digital cameras. Your second camera carries an endorsement from Weird Al's Shutter Shop as number one in his 2002 test of digital cameras. Which endorsement carries the most weight?

A warrant underlies all claims and gives the reader a way to gauge the reliability of the information. In other words, how credible does the reader find the author of the piece? An individual's name alone can offer sufficient warrant to persuade reader to the views of the author. If Mother Teresa said something's true, who could argue? Likewise, I'd give more serious consideration to an essay written on the future of life on Earth written by Stephen Hawking than by Billy Graham, but another person might place more warrant in the opinions of Graham.

When writers consult my editing business for help marketing their nonfiction books or proposals, their authority, meaning the warrant, often means the difference between a sale and none. The more proof, i.e. support, they can offer to establish their qualifications to write their books and promote them, the greater their reliability in the eyes of an agent, a publisher, and the reader.

The warrant not only describes the reliability of the author of a piece or of his sources, it also refers to the relationship between the claim and the support. If the support is sketchy, the warrant is weak for the claim.

Assembling the Pieces

When you sit down to write about an idea, outline your argument to help organize your thinking and to make the most powerful presentation of your ideas. Using my example of an essay on airline seating, here's how it might be outlined:

One-Line Proposition: I propose that airline seating be redesigned according to the physical needs of people and assigned on that basis, eliminating the class system of first class, business, coach, and economy.

Audience: Airline CEOs, stockholders, board of directors.

Lead: I'd probably use an anecdote, based on an actual incident if possible, of travelers with special needs. The best example would be a CEO or VIP who was not in first class and who suffered because of a special need.

Definitions: first class, business, coach, and economy.

Claim—of fact: Supply research such as consumer surveys about dissatisfaction with services; perhaps find lawsuits against airlines by individuals with special needs who win based on violation of the Americans with Disabilities Act or other negligence.

Claim—of policy: Suggest sweeping change in policy from seating according to class and income to seating based on humanitarian concerns.

Support—evidence: Supply cost analysis of profits and losses of the present policy to demonstrate the fiscal crisis; use quotations from cost projections for making seating changes; give projections of profits from innovation, customer satisfaction.

Support—motivational: Build the argument for "doing the right thing," that friendly skies are those that put people first and, paradoxically, get rewarded for that value.

Warrant: Since I have *no* clout for this idea, I should go after endorsements and quotations to use by authorities with clout. For instance, my congressman to the U.S. House of Representatives is Peter DeFazio, who is head of the transportation committee overseeing the airlines. I could interview Mr. DeFazio directly. I could also seek quotations from present and past secretaries of the National Transportation Board and others, either from published materials or by interviews with them.

Conclusion: Reiteration of proposition and a close with a human-interest cameo or quote from one of the special-needs travelers.

Refer to Map 9-1 when you decide to write about ideas where your intent is to persuade your reader to act or believe in a desired way. Map 9-2 offers a list of books about ideas, past and present, in the fields of philosophy, including aesthetics, ethics, and metaphysics.

Writing about ideas—Big Ideas, Important Ideas, and Ideas That Inform—is exciting, sometimes exhilarating. After all, our ability to discuss far-reaching consequences, to entertain the wild and unimaginable, and to share it is one of the greatest gifts of being human. Let the form for presenting your ideas become the vehicle, not the obstacle, to extending your intellectual pursuit of beauty, truth, and excellence.

MAP 9-1

Outlining to Persuade

1. State your proposed idea in one sentence.

2. Define your audience.

3. Decide whether your appeal will be based on logic, ethics, or emotions.

4. Choose a method of organization. (See Map 6-2)

5. Write your lead. (See Map 5-2)

6. Find common ground.

7. Define terms.

8. Introduce a claim based on fact, value, or policy.

9. Concede a point.

10. Develop your argument following your chosen method of organization.

11. Support your claim with factual evidence or with a motivational appeal and avoid name-calling.

12. Build your support depending upon the strength of your warrant.

11. Write a conclusion. (See Map 7-1)

MAP 9-2

Outstanding Books in Four Categories of Ideas

PHILOSOPHY:
The Varieties of Religious Experience: A Study in Human Nature
by William James
The Courage to Be by Paul Tillich
Philosophical Explanations by Robert Nozick
A Brief History of Time: From the Big Bang to Black Holes
by Stephen W. Hawking
The Whole Shebang: A State-of-the-Universe(s) Report
by Timothy Ferris
The Elegant Universe by Brian Greene

AESTHETICS:
√ *The Beauty Myth* by Naomi Wolf
Nature and Culture by Barbara Novak
Dawn to the West: Japanese Literature in the Modern Era
by Donald Keene
Genius: A Mosaic of One Hundred Exemplary Creative Minds
by Harold Bloom
A Beautiful Pageant: African American Theatre, Drama and
Performance in the Harlem Renaissance by David Krasner

ETHICS:
√ *The Future of Life* by Edward O. Wilson
A Theory of Justice by John Rawls
The Culture of Narcissism: American Life in an Age of Diminishing
    Expectations by Christopher Lasch
Christianity, Social Tolerance, and Homosexuality by John Boswell
The Fate of the Earth by Jonathan Schell
The Quality of Mercy: Cambodia, Holocaust, and Modern Conscience
    by William Shawcross
The Moral Animal: Evolutionary Psychology and Everyday Life
by Robert Wright
Overcoming Law by Richard A. Posner

MAP 9-2

Continued

METAPHYSICS:
Consciousness Explained by Daniel C. Dennett
Caught in Fading Light: Mountain Lions, Zen Masters, and Wild Nature by Gary Thorp
The Blank Slate: The Modern Denial of Human Nature by Steven Pinker
A Concealed God: Religion, Science, and the Search for Truth by Stefan Einhorn
Luminous Emptiness: Understanding the Tibetan Book of the Dead by Francesca Fremantle

TEN

Writing About Things

The best and most beautiful things
in life cannot be seen or even touched.
They must be felt in the heart.
                    Helen Keller

IT'S A WONDER THAT Walt Disney didn't create a Large Large World to feature the gizmos, gadgets, products, paraphernalia, objects, tools, machines, and inventions of our lives. We live in an information-laden world that would be unfathomable to preindustrial people. Some of us who are postindustrial still reel from the daily bombardment. Windows, widows, jawbreakers, linebackers, chickens, ducks, doors, s'mores, thesauruses, brontosauruses, changing tables, phone cables, debit cards, playing cards, CDs, PCs, DVDs, SUVs, books, shoes, socks, sacks, packs, ponds, philodendrons, philanthropists, shopping lists, green jeans, blue cheese, black lights, night snacks, magazines, cookie tins, timber, lumber, linoleum, magnolias, mandolins, flowers, flour, things, more things, and more things.

And, it only takes not knowing something to send most of us to places where we know we can find our answers. Increasingly, the first place many look is the Internet. As I explained to my eighty-one-year-old dad, who is now trying to use a computer for the first time, the Internet is "the library of the world." Even so, we continue to seek answers from printed materials of all kinds.

Writing about things boils down to information, including the large subcategory of consumer product and service nonfiction, news, and how-to. Let's examine the structure of each category.

Information

If you want to inform readers, no matter your subject or field of study, the methods of organization covered in chapter six (Map 6-2) offer the best guidance for organizing your research. Select one of these methods such as classification and division, or by importance or complexity. After choosing one method, your job is to create main topics and subtopics if you plan to write an article, and part divisions, chapter divisions, main topics, and subtopics if you plan to write a book.

The clarity of your writing rests on defining terms and vocabulary before you use them. The richness and value of your writing depends on your support with facts, statistics, quotations from authorities, and examples. The warmth of your writing stems from inclusion of people, no matter what your subject is. The excitement of your writing arises from dynamic verbs and concrete nouns.

The best tool for organizing an article or book whose purpose is to inform is often the old-fashioned Roman numeral outline. It is in its glory for material that fits a hierarchy of importance or emphasis. A second kind of outline, which I've used for years, is identical to the one used for genealogy. I prefer it because it's spatial. At a glance, all of the items, such as all main topics, line up vertically and visually—especially if you add color-coding for the hierarchies. The same holds true for the next level—all of the secondary topics, and the next level, and so forth. I may be revealing far too much if I tell you that I outlined many of the lectures and books in graduate school using this "genealogy" flowchart and colored pens.

With either outline, one can easily see where a topic is underdeveloped or overdeveloped. You'll spot where you listed too many examples or too few, compared to other topics or subtopics. Best of all, you can diagnose mistakes in organization in a snap.

Obviously, this advice matches textbooks and educational writing of all kinds. But is it ideal for writing information articles for magazines? As long as you match the style of a magazine in diction, tone, and content, this form of outlining will serve you well.

INFORMATION EXAMPLE

Popular Science has been informing the general public for decades. In the August 2001 issue, Don Sherman wrote a featured informational piece, "Sports Cars Power Up: We Test the Muscle of the Newest Sport Cars on the Track." Here's an analysis of his article's organization:

Lead: Using a journalistic lead with a flair, the writer provides *where*: Willow Springs International Raceway in the desert north of Los Angeles; *why*: a favorite raceway since the '50s; *what*: testing four new sports cars; *who*: the drivers were insignificant and instead the cars were introduced as personalities; *when*: vague but current time.

Definitions: The writer introduces each car and describes its strongest attributes. The reader "meets" a Chevrolet Z06 Corvette, a Porsche Boxster S, a Toyota MR2 Spyder, and an Audi TT Quattro.

Method of Organization: Compare and contrast the four cars' performance. The writer also presented each car within each of the three topics in the order of performance from best to least.

Outline:

    I. Power/Acceleration
       A. Corvette
       B. Boxster
       C. Toyota
       D. Audi

    II. Braking
       A. Corvette
       B. Audi

C. Boxster

D. Toyota

III. Handling
   A. Toyota
   B. Boxster
   C. Audi
   D. Corvette

IV. Combined Test
   A. Description of course
   B. Corvette
   C. Boxster
   D. Audi
   E. Toyota

V. Best/Worst Features of Each Car
   A. Toyota
   B. Boxster
   C. Audi
   D. Corvette

Conclusion: A ta-da about the last point, the combined features of the Corvette: "When the hard charging begins, this is the ride we'd run toward every time." A sidebar, "Test Results," shares the last page of the article and provides a graphic summary of the quantified test results in eleven categories.

Analysis: I've supplied the simplest of outlines for this article, although each of the subtopics, which in most cases are the names of the cars in the order of their performance (from best to worst), could be developed to another level using numbers: A:1,2,3; B: 1,2,3, etc.

I am not a car person, and that is an understatement. Yet, Don Sherman's article, full of technical detail, kept me excited. Why? The writer not only disseminated information, he set up a story. Remember, features benefit from the story pattern and in this case, the purpose of the feature is to compare sports car performance! The reader is held in suspense over which car performed best. If you review the outline above, you'll see that the order changes in each category. It's a race! Who will win? By the end, the author did not select one car over another, because it was not a literal race; it was a comparison of performance features.

This article could have been dry as dust. The author could have adopted a technical-writing voice, like an engineer's, or he could have given us the information, the facts, the statistics, and bored all but the extreme car enthusiast. The writing style kept me, a non-techno, non-car person, excited. Here's an example of what a strong style can do: "The trick is just the right amount of rpm before aggressively engaging the clutch. Get it right and the back of your head kisses the seatback as tires scratch the pavement for purchase and you blast by 60 mph in 4.7 seconds."

See what I mean! You can write about things, you can disseminate information, and you can keep your readers up all night turning pages while their spouses fall asleep with a murder mystery.

Writing to inform can also entertain. It gains power through organization and outlining. As you can see from this example, several methods of organization can be combined successfully. I recommend taking a piece of writing that you admire and analyzing its structure and then modeling it.

Consumer Product and Service

As a particular kind of information article, the new consumer product or service piece, also called the "utility article," appears in almost every magazine and newspaper. The product article not only covers new "things," but also includes reviews of books, movies, videos, plays, art, music, software, and food. The service article covers one or several businesses that offer any form of service, from beauty salons to refrigerator repair. If you decide to focus on the provider of the service, then you are writing a profile and should organize it in a profile pattern (see chapter Eight). If your service piece covers hotels, restaurants, and recreational venues in vacation locations, you'll gain additional help from chapter eleven, "Writing About Places."

After the lead and introduction of the product or service, here is the particular structure common to the body of these articles:

- Description
- History of development
- Evaluation
- Weakness or criticism
- Cost and availability

DESCRIPTION

For a product, especially a new one, describe it fully and describe how it is used. Include all of its features, including any attachments or supplemental uses. Describe the materials, their appearance and feel, and give such specifics as size, durability, model variations, and structural soundness.

For a consumer service, describe the service in detail. For instance, if you want to write about a new massage business in town, include what types of massage are practiced—Swedish, deep tissue, Rolfing. Perhaps the business offers hot tubs, mud packs, facials, or foot massages in addition to full-body massages.

The description of a service piece should also include a sense of the spatial arrangements of the place of business—the décor, lighting, furniture, and ambience. Because all services are people businesses, describe who performs the service, perhaps giving a profile that includes mannerisms, clothing, or nuances of behavior. Make sure to use direct quotations to capture the individual's unique speech pattern as well as to create an active way to offer information.

HISTORY OF DEVELOPMENT

Readers enjoy knowing the genesis of a product and the history of a service. We're all fascinated by inventors and inventions. We love improvements of performance and additions of features. Services are typically the story of one person's vision leading to the present business and clientele.

EVALUATION

The reader entrusts the writer to provide a fair evaluation of a product or service. The choice of publication determines whether your evaluation can be subjective—your experience—or whether it must be limited to consumer surveys or research. Using direct quotations of consumers who have used the product or service keeps the evaluation part of the article from becoming too narrow. Avoid reprinting the manufacturer's superlatives about a product or an owner of a service's testimonials. Otherwise, your article will come across as promotion instead of reporting.

WEAKNESS OR CRITICISM

No product is perfect. No business has 100 percent customer satisfaction. Part of the writer's job in consumer-information writing is to provide a balanced view of the quality of the product or service. When you interview users of the product or service, make sure to include questions that elicit weaknesses and criticism. You should also ask the manufacturer, if that is possible, or the business owner what kinds of customer complaints they have received and where they see room for improvement. Inclusion of this information contributes to balanced reporting.

COST AND AVAILABILITY

Information about cost, availability, store locations, web addresses, phone numbers, and hours of service often work best in a sidebar, a small article that usually appears in a box within the body of the article. If your piece is short or a filler, this information often ends the article.

CONSUMER PRODUCT EXAMPLE

Popular Science is the quintessential gadget magazine. I chose "Palm Reading Made Easy," by senior editor Suzanne Kantra Kirschner, for analysis of the structure of a consumer product article.

History of Development: The writer used the development of PDAs (personal digital assistants) as her summary lead, emphasizing the poor screen resolution, 160 by 160 pixels. She uses an efficient transition from the lead into description of two new PDAs: "Until now, that is."

Description: The reader learns about the "Sony Clié PEG-N710C's 320 by 320 pixel color display and the HandEra 330's 240 by 320 pixel grayscale display." This one line completes the description.

Evaluation: The product evaluation is subjective: "The first thing I noticed is that the test is much easier to read." And, "Both companies tweaked the preloaded software so it makes use of the displays' extra pixels."

Weakness or Criticism: The criticism offered is not of these two new products but of programs that "don't support more than 160 by 160 pixels" because they "look the same." She assures the reader that "an increasing number of applications do support high-resolution displays."

Cost and Availability: The concluding paragraph describes the cost, $500 for the Clié and $350 for the HandEra. The author concludes the article with her endorsement of the additional $50 over former models as worth it for extra pixels.

News

Reporters write news for a living, but freelance writers may also write features, fillers, or information-based news for other publications. We all think we know what news is, but what is it really? Literally, it is information not previously known. When applied to "dailies," news means what's new; typically what has happened within twenty-four hours. News also covers anticipated events that have not yet happened but will (or are scheduled to happen) in the near future.

The shorter the time elapsed since the event being reported on, the harder-edged the writing. The immediacy of "breaking news" necessitates publicizing the facts without delay. The journalistic lead with the five Ws and the H—who, what, where, when, why, how— deals directly with this need.

In terms of organization, even these six elements require ordering. Which should come first? The answer: whichever is most important. To write a hard-edged news lead, address each of the critical questions in order of importance.

Because stories that appear in newspapers must fit available space, and the editor, not the writer, knows what that space is, news writers organize the rest of their stories—after the journalistic lead—in an "inverted pyramid." This pattern describes how the rest of the information of the story should be organized: by *descending* order of importance. In other words, the least important information should appear last in the story.

Another guideline for ordering a news story is to continue the emphasis begun in the lead all of the way through the piece. If the "who" of the story is most important, then continue to develop more information about the people or persons involved in the breaking news. If the "what" is important, then develop more information about the "what," and so forth.

HARD NEWS EXAMPLE

Hard news gets right to the point (remember space constraints and the consumer's need to know). In the following example from an AP news item in the *Los Angeles Times,* I've used brackets to identify what the writer supplies of the five Ws and the H.

Washington [where]—The Food and Drug Administration [who] warned consumers and doctors Monday [when] that kava [what], a popular dietary supplement [defined], carries a "potential risk" of causing severe liver damage [why].

All five Ws were covered in the lead, but the reader must continue reading to learn *how* kava causes liver damage. The second paragraph in this news story reiterates the lead, adding only that the warning came "three months after the FDA asked doctors to review cases for links between kava and liver problems."

The reader still doesn't know what health condition kava treats. However, the writer stays true to one focus: emphasizing the "what," the warning. The third paragraph describes that someone might take it for "sleeplessness, stress, anxiety, and menopausal symptoms."

Staying true to warning the consumer, the writer begins the third paragraph by quoting a FDA spokeswoman who repeats the warning and states that the exact biological explanation of the link remains unknown.

The fourth paragraph supplies information about the events that brought kava to the attention of the FDA: "The herbal supplement has been connected to more than twenty-five cases of liver-related injuries in other countries, FDA officials said." Continuing in the same vein, the fifth paragraph describes the one U.S. case where a woman required a liver transplant after taking kava. The article could have used this information for a lead or for placement as the second sentence in the article. While it is impossible to know exactly why the writer (or his editor) did not lead with the twenty-five cases and one liver transplant, it could be that to do so would elevate concern before more evidence of the danger.

Only in the sixth and last paragraph of the news item does the reader get the least important information relative to the "warning" slant. In this paragraph, the reader learns that the plant is indigenous to South America and ranks ninth in sales of herbal supplements.

In the last two sentences, the reader learns what symptoms to look for: jaundice and brown urine or nausea, weakness, and tiredness. Since these symptoms can stem from causes other than taking kava, the writer (or editor) might have decided that to put them first—as the most-important warning—risked unnecessary alarm to the public. Instead, by placing emphasis on the warning about kava as a supplement, the writer may have acted more responsibly.

SOFT NEWS EXAMPLE

Nearly every consumer magazine includes a regular news feature. Since magazines typically come out monthly, bimonthly, or quarterly, the news they print has less urgency. In the following example, also a consumer alert, notice the "softer edge," the informational tone versus the hard-news tone. The article, "Ticked Off," by Melinda Leader, appeared in *Ladies' Home Journal.*

> Good news about Lyme disease [what], the potentially debilitating tick-borne illness [definition] that strikes 16,000 people [magnitude of problem] each year. Researchers [who] are gaining a better understanding of how the insects transmit disease-carrying bacteria to humans [what], which may lead to a more effective vaccine in the next decade [why].

In this lead, the journalistic question "when" is not terribly relevant. The writer includes "each year" and "next decade," which is far different than a FDA warning that implies we should stop using kava right now.

The second paragraph of this news article expands on the lead by substituting specific details for the prior generalities: "scientists at University of North Carolina at Chapel Hill" for "researchers," "Lymerix" for "vaccines" and so on.

After completing the news portion of the article, the last half of the short article gives consumer information about who should get the vaccine, how to protect yourself in tick-infested areas, and how to dress before going hiking. The last paragraph concludes with symptoms of Lyme disease, the present treatment, and ends with an 800 number and web address "for more information."

How-To

One of the most popular of articles (or books) to write, the how-to for things versus the how-to for people and relationships is straightforward and concrete. How-to writing confers the mantle of authority to the writer, who instructs the reader using the second-person pronoun "you." The spirit of how-to writing is optimistic and encouraging.

Your lead for how-to writing needs to reflect this "you-can-do-it" promise. The ideal methods of organization for the body of a how-to are order of ascending complexity (from simple to complex) or step-by-step in order of construction or creation. Occasionally, an ideal method of organization will be an analogy, if you can use something familiar to offer instructions for something unfamiliar.

A definition of terms and an explanation of tools is necessary or you'll drive your novice reader nuts! What is the difference between a pipe, a monkey, a socket, a crescent, and a double-ended wrench? Or, if you tried to follow a recipe that told you to shirr the eggs, braise the meat, or fold in the egg whites, would you know what to do? Define and explain!

One of the additions to this kind of how-to article is a materials and tools list, which you can summarize in a sidebar or in the introduction, after the lead. Here are some other tips for effective how-to writing:

- Use concrete examples. "From airports to fisheries, Border collies, the working dog, have been the most effective deterrent to unwanted birds." Not: "Industries facing losses due to birds have had to find innovative solutions."

- Use specific descriptions. Panther Creek Cellars Pinot Noir, not red wine.

- Use the terminology appropriate to the subject or field. "At the climax, the protagonist reached the story goal and, in the denouement, realized he had found home." Not, "When things got really bad, the dude pounded the evil guys and, when the dust settled, he was really, really glad he didn't have to budge."

- Use facts based on research. "According to the Oregon Department of Health, 10 percent of all bats test positive for rabies." Not, "The risk of getting rabies from bats is low."

- Avoid the phrases, "I think" and "I suggest." Write "Heat the oven to 350 degrees," not, "I suggest that you heat the oven to 350 degrees."

This book is a how-to-write book. Concrete examples from magazines and books follow instruction in form and structure. Instead of introducing leads and defining what they are, for instance, the explanation of leads included descriptions of specific types. Terminology particular to the field of writing peppers this book. I've based the instruction in this book on researched facts and on professional experience. I've avoided "I think" and "I suggest" because the opinion or suggestion of the writer of any how-to article or book is assumed and implied.

FOOD RECIPE

Writing about food is a particular type of how-to article. Begin with a mouthwatering lead that also has the "you-can-do-it" promise. Tell your reader why they'll enjoy the dishes and why they are easy to prepare. Give examples of your featured food as a part of a whole meal. After your lead, list your ingredients in the order of their use. If your recipe involves the use of any unusual cooking equipment, consider an equipment list as well.

In the body of the article, provide step-by-step instructions for preparation of the food. Be specific about the size of pots, pans, bowls, cooking time, and variations. More than for any other kind of instructional writing, recipe instructions are short. Imagine your reader in the kitchen using your recipe. Give one direction at a time—in the right order. This implies that you have tested your recipe, which is a very important step to take if you don't want egg on your face—so to speak.

At the end of your recipe, make sure to indicate how many people your portions serve. Many publications also require an indication of total calories per serving and possibly the quantity of fats, carbohydrates, and sodium in milligrams.

All but the simplest and shortest food-recipe articles include reflections of the writer's personality. Some articles or cookbooks may include "creative writing," such as a travel experience when the writer first discovered the recipe or a personal experience that adds a dimension and "flavor" to the piece. There is a definite blending of food-recipe articles, personal essays, and travel writing. Your best guideline is to model the publications where you intend to submit your articles. You may also want to consult chapters eight and eleven if you want to write more than a basic how-to food-recipe piece.

Sidebars

Any of the forms of writing about things is suitable for this most versatile staple of nonfiction writing, the sidebar. Sidebars are short, often abbreviated, articles, lists, charts, graphs, or quizzes that are typeset in boxes and appear within the text on a page. They provide visual relief from blocks of text, they are eye-catching and stimulating, and easy to read. They offer writers a way to provide detailed information that would otherwise interfere with the flow of prose or be downright boring. They also add money to your pocket from any publication that pays by the word.

Renamed to correspond with the compass metaphor, the maps in this book are sidebars. Whenever you have technical details, "factoids" and stats, lists or resources, background information, or related but separate information, put it in a sidebar.

WRITING about "things"—information, news, and how-to—is the backbone of nonfiction writing. If you would like a career as a freelance writer, writing about things will put bread on your table. And, if you also write a food article about the bread and a how-to piece about the table, you'll generate income and a tax deduction at the same time.

ELEVEN

Writing About Places

*Spirit of place! It is for this we travel, to surprise its subtlety;
and where it is a strong and dominant angel, that place, seen
once, abides entire in the memory of all its own accidents,
its habits, its breath, its name.*

Alice Meynell

IN THE MID-1960s, my high-school humanities teacher peered over heavy black glasses and made this prophecy: "You will be the first generation to travel the globe. Air travel will become like taking the bus." Sara Moss Phillips called it right: we're travelin', baby.

According to the U.S. Census, a baby boomer turns fifty every 7.5 seconds and, by 2005, the majority of the 76 million boomers will be in the fifty- to seventy-year-old age group. The consequences of a retired and mobile population of this size, one with relative affluence, is a burgeoning travel and leisure industry. As the industry expands, its accommodation to travelers' needs also expands. This means that leisure and travel is not limited to seniors or near-seniors; families with children and pets find places that welcome their business as well.

For anyone who likes to write about places, the markets for travel, nature, and outdoor writing can be expected to flourish. The narrative and "spiritual" travel book category also continues to expand. Open nearly any magazine and you'll find a feature on one or many vacation spots.

HOW-TO BOOKS ON TRAVEL WRITING

Travel Writing by L. Peat O'Neil

How to Make a Living as a Travel Writer by Susan Farewell

Writing About Travel by Brian Anderson

Teach Yourself Travel Writing by Cynthia Dial

Travel Writing in Fiction and Fact by Jane Edwards

Travel Photography by Susan McCartney

The Best American Science and Nature Writing 2001 edited by Edward O. Wilson

The Best American Travel Writing 2000 edited by Bill Bryson

The Earth Speaks by Steve Van Matre, Gwen Frostic (illustrator), and Bill Weiler

At first glance, travel, nature, outdoor writing, and the travel memoir appear to have their own rules and conventions. A closer look reveals the underlying "bones"; the structure of these forms of travel writing match the methods of organization and patterns already covered in prior chapters. However, writing about places also has a style and vocabulary all its own. Because the focus of this book is primarily on structure, I strongly recommend that you study the style of the travel and nature genres by reading them.

Writing about places takes a myriad of forms. Here we'll be looking at five distinct categories: travel essays, travel news and information, travel how-to, travel research, and nature and the outdoors. Many of these categories have a number of subcategories as well. If you feel drawn to writing about places, you have a cornucopia of choices.

Travel Essays

When you decide to write about your own experiences while traveling, review the methods of organization and patterns covered in chapter eight, "Writing About People." A well-developed slant and a compelling lead are critical for success in this genre of writing, simply because the same territory has been well covered by prior writers.

Most travel essays, also called travel narratives, fall into seven categories:

- Me and Joe
- Travel humor
- Diary/journal/letters
- Memoir
- Literary/mood piece
- Narrative book
- Photographic

ME AND JOE

This funny title has been bestowed upon the type of essay written in the first person that describes the writer's travel experience— often with "Joe," a male, female, or traveling companion. "Joe" can be the writer's spouse, friend, pet . . . the possibilities are many. When working in this form, pay attention to your building blocks—slant, promise, and theme—and match style to the publication to which you will submit. "Me and Joe" essays are typically light and may include a sprinkle of humor. The quintessential "me and Joe" book is *Travels with Charley,* by John Steinbeck, Charley being his poodle. More recently, *Under the Tuscan Sun: At Home in Italy,* by Frances Mayes, describes her experiences shared with her husband, Ed, after moving into a farmhouse in Tuscany. Combining the "me and Joe" form and adventuresome spirit with the serious topic of financial commentary, Jim Rogers's *Investment*

Biker recounts his motorcycle trip around the world with his girl-friend, Tabitha, and his observations about world economies.

TRAVEL HUMOR

This form of writing about place, as the name implies, combines humor as a slant with a travel situation. If you have traveled at all, you have probably encountered some unexpected situations that strike you now, if not then, as humorous, and could be ideal for a humorous travel essay. When I was seventeen, for instance, I was detained at Checkpoint Charlie by an East German border guard because my tour leader failed to put my name and social security number on the list of Americans in our group. In 1967, it was not good to be an East German attempting escape to the West. For over an hour, I answered the guard's questions—in English. In exasperation, I decided to shift to German on the chance that the friendly gesture would endear me to him. It worked! As soon as I spoke German, a grin split his face and I was allowed to pass into West Berlin. Years later, a German woman listened to my tale and nearly doubled over with laughter at my conclusions. "Your accent is so bad," she told me, "as soon as you spoke German, he knew for sure you were an American." I have not yet written this as a travel essay, but it is ideal for one. An example of travel humor in a short form is "Adventures of the Frisco Kid," by Michael Lewis in *Gourmet* (March '02).

Travel humor, like any humor writing, is difficult to sustain for an entire book, yet many writers do so with aplomb. Veteran travel writer Tim Cahill wrote about his utterly hilarious and insane adventure of driving from the southern tip of South America to the northern-most point in Alaska—in 23.5 days—in *Road Fever: A High-Speed Travelogue.* Bill Bryson's *A Walk in the Woods,* as well as his other travel narratives are wonderful examples of travel humor. British author Paul Mayle, in *A Year in Provence,* offers a superb example of wit and charm that fits both travel humor and the next category, travel journal, because of its organization by month.

DIARY/JOURNAL/LETTERS

The travel diary is a form of memoir. The travel diary or journal, sometimes referred to as "mile by mile," or a collection of letters, is a difficult kind of writing. Its progressive date entries may render the piece "episodic," meaning that it unfolds as a string of unrelated episodes with no sense of cohesion. Two factors can overcome these obstacles: exceptional writing or celebrity. Readers will always be interested in the private thoughts and observations of someone famous. If you are not famous and you want to market your travel diary, your writing had better be original and leap off the page. A famous example is *Journals: Early Fifties Early Sixties,* by Allen Ginsberg, also a braided narrative of stream of consciousness, free verse, anecdotes and remembrances, poems, and even doodles and drawings. *Adrift: Seventy-Six Days Lost at Sea,* by Steven Callahan, chronicles the day-by-day events of survival while adrift at sea in his inflatable raft. An example of a book of letters about place—and much more—is *Dear Mom: A Sniper's Vietnam,* by Joseph Ward, featuring letters sent home revealing his experiences as a marine scout sniper during the Vietnam War.

MEMOIR

Memoir is, of course, writing about people, but the travel memoir is a particular kind of writing about place deserving mention all its own. What distinguishes the travel memoir from the usual memoir is that the place and events are a catalyst for a deeper understanding of self, which is fully developed. Fortunately, writers in this genre of travel writing have not had to compete with domination by celebrity authors. There are so many wonderful examples; I've listed many in the resource box on page 146.

LITERARY/MOOD PIECE

A lot of the success of selling travel essays involves the creation (or the re-creation) of atmosphere and mood. When your writing succeeds in transporting your reader to the place you describe, giving

OUTSTANDING TRAVEL MEMOIRS

Into Thin Air and *Into the Wild* by Jon Krakauer

Blue Highways: A Journey into America and *River Horse* by William Least Heat-Moon

An Unspoken Hunger; Refuge: An Unnatural History of Family and Place; and Red: Passion and Patience in the Desert by Terry Tempest Williams

The Tiger Ladies: A Memoir of Kashmir by Sudha Koul

The Hacienda by Lisa St. Aubin de Teran

Pilgrim Heart: The Inner Journey Home by Sarah York

Deep Water Passage: A Spiritual Journey at Midlife by Ann Linnea

There Are Mountains to Climb by Jean Deeds

Riding to Jerusalem by Bettina Selby

The House on Dream Street: Memoir of an American Woman in Vietnam by Dana Sachs

No Mountain Too High: A Triumph over Breast Cancer by Andrea Gabbard

them the vicarious experience of being there, you have created a mood piece. Mood pieces such as those appearing in *Condé Nast Traveler*, for instance, fall into the category of literary writing—as contrasted with mainstream writing style. Literary writing features originality of perception and expression, writing that is evocative and often symbolic, and a "greater" distance from the experience than the "me and Joe" essay. Literary writing reflects a maturity of expression, which is often conveyed through complex sentence structure and subtle nuances of language. Literary mood essays and books may be memoirs or travel narratives. *Southwestern Homelands,* by William Kittredge, offers literary writing about place. Barry Lopez writes evocative literary books about place that are distinctly "atmospheric"; *Arctic Dreams* is one of his most famous works. The name of the author Paul Theroux is practically synonymous with literary travel writing. *The Old Patagonian Express* and *The Great Railway Bazaar* are but two of his many bestselling books. David James Duncan writes literary prose about water in *The River Why* and *My Story as Told by Water.*

NARRATIVE BOOK

Written in first person, the travel narrative conveys the subjectivity and intimacy of the diary and the "me and Joe" essay with the depth and sophistication of the mood piece. Yet, it is its own kind of writing. The book keeps its focus on the place and the theme. In that sense, it is not a travel memoir where the focus remains on the author's interior experiences and discoveries as developed by the place. Both a political and travel narrative is *From Beirut to Jerusalem,* by Thomas Friedman. *Walking the Bible,* by Bruce Feiler, about his 10,000-mile trek in Moses' footsteps with archaeologist and travel companion Avner Goren might also be considered a "me and Joe" book. *A Whale Hunt: How a Native-American Village Did What No One Thought They Could,* by Robert Sullivan, chronicles the author's two years spent with the Makah people as they prepare for a first hunt in nearly seventy years.

PHOTOGRAPHIC

When you have outstanding photographs accompanied by a first-person account of your travel experiences, you have a photographic essay. The key to this work is "outstanding photographs." They sell the work; not the writing, although the writing is obviously important. These books are very expensive because of the cost of producing high-quality photographs. *In Response to Place: Photographs from the Nature Conservancy's Last Great Places,* edited by Andy Grundberg with a foreword by Terry Tempest Williams, is one example. Another example that has more writing, by Claude Levi-Strauss as translated by Sylvia Modelski, is *Saudades Do Brasil (Nostalgia for Brazil): A Photographic Memoir.*

News and Information

The purpose to inform dominates writing about places for obvious reasons: readers have a high interest in learning as much as they can about a place they intend to visit. Like other information-based writing, there are many types of information pieces including:

- News Peg
- Historical
- Roundup
- Service
- Food Recipe
- Destination
- Special Interest

NEWS PEG

When a place is in the news or you can find a timing tie-in related to a place, this tie-in is the article's news peg. Do you remember when the Olympics were in Salt Lake City? Freelance writers and reporters reported on the Mormons and their religion, on places where alcohol was served, on recreation areas, on the history of settling Utah, and on all manner of pieces about life in Salt Lake City.

Another way to find a news peg is to pay attention to anniversaries of historic events related to a location. In the Pacific Northwest where I live, the anniversaries of Mt. St. Helen's eruption will always find an audience eager for updates on the flora and fauna, on recent volcanic activity, and on campgrounds and side attractions.

Last of all, you may find a news peg related to a person. Whenever someone makes the news, travel articles about their hometown, state, or country may suddenly become in demand.

HISTORICAL

Every location has pioneers, settlers, heroes, heroines, the notorious, and the evil. Buildings hold secrets of the past and artifacts fill museums.

One of the decisions you have to make is to select a time period and region, or location, you want to cover. You might let a historical event offer a timing tie-in as well as a specific, versus broad location. For instance, I could use the anniversary of the arrival of Lewis and Clark at the end of the Oregon Trail, the eruption of Mt. St. Helens (in southwest Washington), or the death of the Olympic runner Steve Prefontaine. To put all three of these historic events in one article, the scope would have to be very wide, such as a roundup of the major events in the history of the Pacific Northwest. It wouldn't be appropriate to describe, or even mention, all three in an article about my city, Eugene. However, if I chose the last one, the death of Prefontaine, I might also profile Bill Bowerman, Prefontaine's University of Oregon coach, *and* Nike, which used Bowerman's shoe designs as its prototypes and whose history parallels Prefontaine's career.

Your decisions all go back to your purpose, what difference you wish to make, and your slant. Because I'm more couch potato than sports buff, I'd be more likely to select a roundup of writers and related sights and events. Perhaps I'd cover some of the pioneer women writers, locations of their diaries, essays, and books, and the regions in Oregon where they settled. If you're a history buff, the historical angle to travel writing could be made to order for you.

ROUNDUP

As a variation of the consumer-service article, the roundup offers the reader a profile of many items in a particular locale. Those items might be hotels or bed-and-breakfasts, restaurants, beaches, museums, or any other grouping in a specific area. The idea is to "round up" the options and offer them in one article. As you might

expect, these pieces require lots of research, but they usually find a
ready reception.

SERVICE

This kind of article is no different from the consumer-service article
mentioned in chapter ten, "Writing About Things," where the
writer profiles and reviews a service. However, the service examined
for travel writing will be a particular hotel, rail trip, birding or
wildlife outing, or a flight tour. Besides providing the obvious information and evaluation of the service, make sure to include directions for getting to the location.

FOOD RECIPE

One of the great pleasures of being a tourist in a place we've never
been is sampling the food. You could do a roundup article about a
location's eateries or its local beverages, but you can also write a
food-recipe article. The difficulty with this type of article is getting
that family recipe for mole from the Yucatecan restaurateur, for
example, as well as permission to use it. Consider doing an interview of the chef or owner in addition to securing one or several
recipes. That way, you have the option of doing a profile and perhaps several articles. Another popular form of writing about food
and travel is the travel essay, with emphasis on food. Pick up a copy
of any *Gourmet* magazine, for instance, and you'll see exemplary
examples of this type of writing.

DESTINATION

The destination article offers to cover *everything* related to one location. As such, it is one of the most difficult information pieces
to write. Readers who have never been to St. Petersburg—Florida
or Russia—want to know what the whole city and surrounding
area offers in terms of lodging, food, sightseeing, history, shopping,
and recreation. Because these pieces must be both comprehensive
and entertaining, they generally have to hit the highlights and sac-

rifice depth. However, destination pieces are popular because they put a place in the limelight.

SPECIAL INTEREST

When a writer selects a subject and pairs it with a location, it is called a special-interest piece. Let's say that you love to go on walks. Your travel article about Seattle might feature walking trails, walking events, and Seattle champions in walking competitions. You'll still want to include other things to do and see while in Seattle and use a sidebar for lodging, for instance, but your slant is a subject slant. You're writing to serve a special interest, and therefore, you have already targeted particular publications.

How-To

The how-to article for travel, also called "travel advice," is identical to any other self-help article, and you can use that structure. The only difference is the travel slant. For instance, you could use the journalistic five Ws as the focus of your advice: who—how to travel with babies; what—how to pack a suitcase; where—how to find the best parks; when—how to get the most sightseeing for your available time; and why—how to understand foreign political structures. Travelers always want to know how to save money, reduce stress, and have the most fun.

Nature and Outdoors

While travel pieces are aimed at the tourist, nature and outdoors articles, essays, and books serve a different audience. Readers of nature and environmental writing seek enhanced appreciation and understanding of nature—rocks, minerals, trees, plants, flowers, and animals of all kinds. They may be interested in geography, geology, and archaeology as well as ecology and the environmental

**HELPFUL BOOKS ON NATURE
AND OUTDOOR WRITING**

The Incomparable Land: A Guide to American Nature Writing
edited by Thomas J. Lyon (a history of the genre)

The Alphabet of Trees: A Guide to Nature Writing
edited by Christian McEwen and Mark Statman

Writing Naturally: A Down-to-Earth Guide to Nature Writing
by David Peterson and H. Emerson Blake

At Home on This Earth: Two Centuries of U.S. Women's Nature Writing
edited by Lorraine Anderson and Thomas Edwards

*Keeping a Nature Journal: Discover a Whole New Way of Seeing the
World Around You* by Clare Walker Leslie and Charles E. Roth

impact of man. The author acts as the readers' guide, naturalist, and sometimes as their conscience.

Nature writing often requires an ability to understand and interpret the findings of science. If you do not have the education or career credentials for writing about these subjects, you can rely on others who are experts, or you can write as a lay naturalist, an astute observer. However, the onus of accuracy is upon you. Although nature writing rests on science, the essay form leaves plenty of room for the writer's interaction with the environment, including one's inner emotional landscape as well as the outer landscape of the setting. One of the best ways to improve your skill in nature and outdoor writing is to read examples of it, as well as books on how to write this specialized kind of writing. The resource box lists some of these books.

In contrast, readers of outdoors writing seek practical advice and entertainment about exploration and fun in the outdoors. These articles cover hunting, sports, camping, and vehicles including RVs, motorcycles, and ATVs, guns, archery, fishing, photographic, camping and skiing equipment, and any other product connected with the outdoors.

You can also write outdoor essays such as the whitewater raft trip from hell, motorcycling across Death Valley, or scuba diving off the Great Barrier Reef. Obviously, you want to play up the excitement and drama inherent in the experience. The story pattern may offer an effective way to organize your adventure. Make full use of fictional techniques such as dialogue, setting, sensory detail, and scene structure. An out-of-print book, still available used, that covers the full range of outdoor writing is *How to Write for the Outdoors Magazines: A Concise Guide to Writing Fishing, Hunting, and Other Outdoor Articles,* by Jim Capossela.

While you can rely upon the structures mentioned in prior chapters, nature and outdoors writing, like travel writing, is a specialty. As such you will need to either interview experts or become one yourself. To help you with preparations, Map 11-1 lists research items for the intentional tourist writer.

WRITING about places is a uniquely rewarding specialty among the writing genres. You get to go places. Many of us like to travel and see new places, but the travel freelancer goes with a mission—and gets to write off his expenses. It's not a field for every writer, but if it's yours, the world is your oyster.

MAP 11-1

Researching the Travel Piece
Before, During, and After Your Trip

1. Read magazines where you hope to publish. Also read travel guides, articles, and web sites about your destination.

2. Query ahead of time. Take a copy of your query, a letter of assignment (if you get one), and a copy of the magazine where you hope to publish. You can show both of these to help gain interviews and information.

3. Research the history of your destination and make a list of important events and dates. Also list historic figures and contemporary personalities of the locale.

4. Identify what the region is famous for in the past and in the present, including its architecture, art, music, landmarks, and people.

5. Organize your research by age interest and cover all ages or the group for which you want to write.

6. Pack pens and notepads, plastic bags you can seal (good for lots of things), camera and film, batteries, tape recorder, and an electronic "personal digital assistant" if you wish.

7. List modes of travel, and make sure you get information on costs, schedules, and locations for trains, bikes, boats, shuttles, streetcars, or subways.

8. Research places to stay. Take notes on the costs of lodging: budget, economy, business, and luxury. When you are on location, get evaluations of the quality of various accommodations from people who have stayed there.

MAP 11-1

Continued

9. Search out locally known restaurants and nightspots in addition to the usual tourist spots. Collect menus and recipes. Ask locals where they most like to eat. Take notes on how much the meals cost.

10. When you arrive at your destination, contact an area newspaper and tap a city or community editor's insider knowledge. Get the scoop on local personalities and consider lining up interviews. Take an editor to lunch and you may also make a friend.

11. Gather brochures of tours, especially ones unique to the location.

12. Visit or gather information about noted gardens, wildlife preserves, or sanctuaries.

13. When you get home, fill in your notes and enter or upload them into a computer file as soon as possible. Capture the details and the aura of the trip before they fade.

SOUTH

Troubleshooting and
Problem Solving

TWELVE

Troubleshooting and Problem Solving

No exile at the South Pole or on the summit of Mont Blanc separates us more effectively from others than the practice of a hidden vice.

Marcel Proust

MANY YEARS AGO, my friend Stew and I had the editing equivalent of dueling banjos. I edited my manuscript meticulously, checking for problems with structure, logic, content, clarity, style, grammar, punctuation, and spelling. Stew would do the same with his manuscript. We'd meet. I'd thrust my manuscript into his hands, certain that he would be hard-pressed to find a single mistake. He'd give me his perfect manuscript and, with wry, knowing smiles, we'd part. When we met again to return each other's manuscript, both of them dripped with bloodred ink according to our "take no prisoners" agreement.

All writers are wed to their creations, even when they have honed objective self-editing skills. Murphy's Law rules over final drafts. The moment they have been mailed and are irretrievable, you're going to glance down at the first page of your original and see a goober. That mistake will be one so stupid that you'll feel like an idiot. The catch-22 is that no writer can see his own work objectively.

That being true, it's still important to learn how to troubleshoot and problem solve. The most common reason why manuscripts are not accepted for publication is that they weren't ready. They had too many errors. In South, you'll learn how to cast a net to catch many of your own errors. Editing is one of those lifelong skills. If you continue to develop editing alongside your writing, you'll become professional at both. One day, in your equivalent of the dueling banjos with an opponent of Stew's caliber, maybe, just maybe, your manuscript will come back untouched—the ultimate achievement!

In the meantime, if you can find, start, or join a good critique group, you can gain invaluable feedback, including constructive criticism, identification of your strengths, and marketing ideas. Unless you do the equivalent of winning the lottery—you find the perfect critique group—expect to put out effort. Like building a good marriage, becoming a high-functioning critique group also takes work. Because so many writers are members in groups, I've written several columns on resolving problems that occur and threaten to turn a good group into none at all. These columns are available as archived tips at my web site, www.elizabethlyon.com. Whether or not you belong to a critique group, the following guidelines should help you with revision.

Nonfiction writing shares problems across the board with any other writing, but it also has areas of difficulty peculiar to it. Likewise, each type or category of nonfiction writing presents its own challenges for revision and polishing. This section of the book will address special problems related to:

- Concept
- Basic Structure
- Writing About People
- Writing About Ideas
- Writing About Things
- Writing About Places

Concept

Even when you know better, it's easy to jump into writing on a subject you're excited about without giving thought to what you want to accomplish and how you plan to go about it. Errors in concept rank at the top of the list. Use the following review of the early chapters of this book to troubleshoot your manuscripts. Answer questions 1–15 below about your writing.

PURPOSE

When a writer isn't clear which purpose is primary, the reader has the extra burden of figuring out what the writer intends. Confusion and work are the last things you want to foist on your reader. For each piece of writing, identify your primary purpose.

1. My primary purpose in this manuscript is to:
   A. entertain
   B. inform/instruct
   C. persuade
   D. inspire

PROMISE

Each piece of writing makes a promise to the reader and fulfills it by the conclusion of the piece. Depending upon the type of writing and the purpose, it may be a physical, intellectual, emotional/social, or spiritual promise.

2. The promise in my piece is:
   A. physical (such as survival, basic needs)
   B. intellectual (such as tolerance, progress)
   C. emotional/social (such as belonging, responsibility)
   D. spiritual (such as faith, trust)

THEME

Promise and theme are closely allied. Once you know your promise, you can express it as a thematic statement: "Trust is the basis of all enduring relationships." You should be able to express the theme of your piece in one sentence.

3. My theme is: (finish the sentence).

MAKING A DIFFERENCE

A new way of looking at writing, making a difference is an opportunity to consciously know and express your deepest values. With each piece of writing, you can determine how you want your reader to be changed. Knowing this ahead of time (or after writing a first draft) will help you develop clarity and impact.

4. In this piece of writing, the difference I wish to make in my reader's experience is: (finish the sentence).

READERS

The audience for your writing will be different depending upon what you write and how you write it. You can miss the mark if you don't know your intended reader and use the wrong diction, slant, word choice, or complexity, and if you assume a certain knowledge and sophistication.

5. The profile for my intended reader for this piece of writing includes:
   A. gender
   B. age range
   C. educational level
   D. social class
   E. other considerations for this piece of writing

PLACEMENT

You should have an idea which newspaper, magazine, journal, or shelving location (for a book) best fits your piece of writing.

6. The most ideal publications (or bookstore shelves) for my manuscript are: (fill in blank).

CATEGORIZING YOUR WORK

If you're unclear which type of article, essay, or book you're writing, you'll risk structuring it improperly. I've had many an editing client who thought he was writing a self-help book, for instance, but the organization and diction was actually academic or technical. I've had to struggle to learn how a column is different from instructional writing. Many writers confuse memoir with autobiography or family history.

7. I am writing:
   A. an article
   B. an essay
   C. a book

8. I am writing:
   A. Information
      1. news and reports
      2. investigative
      3. consumer product
      4. consumer service
      5. technical
   B. How-to
      1. about everyday things
      2. self-help
      3. technical
   C. Features
   D. Profiles

1. Q&A

   E. Columns
   F. Opinions
   G. Personal experience
      1. as told to
      2. confession
      3. inspirational
      4. nostalgia
      5. humor
      6. memoir
      7. autobiography
      8. biography/family history

SLANT

The kiss of death for any piece of writing is a lack of slant. Slant defines the way you intend to approach your manuscript. Without one—one of the most common failings—you lose your chance to select the content and emphasis of your subject. Your purpose begins to define a slant, but one of the fifteen additional ways to make your writing unique is nearly always essential to publication, not to mention clarity of subject development.

9. For this piece of writing, I am using the following slant(s):

   adrenaline   numbers
   amazement   promises
   brand-new   secrets
   detailed   sexy
   funny   superlatives
   location   unexpected
   money   combination
   newsy

Basic Structure

Because form and structure exist to give spirit a container of expression, spirit can take over and send a writer off a cliff into a free fall until land reminds him of the laws of physics. Mangled or missing structure is the case more often than the exception, possibly because it's simply less fun planning than writing.

LEADS

Lots of things can go wrong with leads. Besides not having one, you may not have chosen a type of lead that fits the piece you're writing. You may get into a rut and use the same types for everything. You can diagnose other problems with your leads:

10. I have a problem writing leads that are:
    A. lackluster
    B. a cliché
    C. lacking emotion
    D. too long
    E. lack theme or promise

BEGINNINGS

The lead just gets your piece started. The rest of the beginning requires more development before you get into the "guts" of your material. The next item will help you diagnose problems with your beginning.

11. I have a problem with writing weak beginnings that:
    A. fail to describe the subject
    B. omit a theme
    C. miss using a transition into the body
    D. fail to include real or anecdotal people, the application of subject

TRANSITIONS

Transitions hold writing together and they also contribute to internal logic. Internal logic refers to the way that language makes sense. If your transitions are abrupt, then the problem may be a call to build skill. The problem may also signal omitted material or material that is in the wrong order. Double-check your transitions between the beginning and the body of your piece and also between sections, paragraphs, and sentences.

12. The type(s) of transitions I have *not* used and should include:
    A. transitional words and phrases
    B. repetition of words and phrases
    C. repetition of sentence structure or a grammatical element
    D. echoes of subject or mood

Plan to read your writing aloud after each revision. Spot-check specifically for hitches and bumps. Diagnose your problem. Is it related to transitions, logic, or the writing itself?

METHODS OF ORGANIZATION

The longer your work, the more likely it is that you will use more than one method of organization. Even so, you should select one overall structure to lend unity and cohesiveness to your writing.

13. My piece uses the following method(s) of organization:
    A. analysis
    B. analogy
    C. cause/effect
    D. chronology
    E. classification and division
    F. comparison/contrast
    G. inductive or deductive
    H. order of importance or complexity

I. problem/solution
J. sequential
K. story

DEFINITIONS

Another structural element is definition of terms. Remember, your expertise makes you prone to blind spots. It will be hard to recognize what terms and ideas your readers might not understand. Go through your manuscript searching for terms and defining them.

EXAMPLES AND SPECIFICITY

Examples are another basic element of nonfiction. Reread your manuscript to spot generalities. Revise and support them with specific examples, evidence, facts, statistics, or anecdotes.

CHECKLIST FOR PARAGRAPHS

Each paragraph should state your topic, define your terms, demonstrate your support, summarize your findings or conclusions, and make a transition to the next paragraph.

14. Use this check-off list. Do your paragraphs:
   A. State
   B. Define
   C. Demonstrate
   D. Summarize
   E. Transition to next paragraph

CONCLUSIONS

Check your endings as well. The most common error with conclusions is petering out. Some writers believe they solve the problem by omitting a conclusion altogether. With your ending, you have a chance to "seal the deal," to affirm the reader's good judgment in trusting you.

15. I have concluded my piece by using:
   A. summary
   B. callback to the beginning
   C. thematic statement
   D. encouragement
   E. a quotation
   F. an emotional "ta-da"

Writing About People

POINT OF VIEW

One of the first considerations in writing about people in any form is viewpoint—who is telling the story. It doesn't matter if you are writing an article, essay, or book, and it doesn't matter what your purpose is or your style of writing. You can't avoid viewpoint considerations and their potential problems.

Your choices are two: subjective or objective viewpoint. In terms of "distance," the subjective viewpoint creates a sense of intimacy, while objective viewpoint creates a faraway feeling. Distance from what or whom? From the subject and from the reader, and sometimes from the self.

Pronouns reflect the various viewpoints. You can choose first person (I, me, us, our), second person (you), or third person (he, she, they, their). First person is considered intense, subjective, and emotionally hot. It is the natural choice for memoir, autobiography, and most personal-experience essays. The reader is the center of attention for second person. It is the favored point of view for instructional material, advice, and sometimes admonishment! It is intimate without being intense—unless the "voice" of the author is authoritarian or controlling instead of instructive. Second person is subjective, even if the focus of the writing is on an objective subject, because the relationship represented by second person—

author talking to reader—is subjective. The emotional temperature of second person is warm.

Third person can be subjective or objective. For instance, when used for an "as told to" personal-experience essay, third person is subjective and warm. When used for news and information, third person is objective and cool.

Although you can, and sometimes should, mix points of view within one manuscript, this may cause problems. You may cause an abrupt transition or choppy prose. A change from third person to second person within one sentence will yank the reader from an objective overview into subjective intimacy. On the other hand, overuse of one point of view, especially first person and second person, will wear out your reader's ear.

CHARACTERIZATION

We tend to think that characterization applies only to fiction writing. Yet, it is a central part of effective nonfiction writing. In fact, the main failing of "people stories" is insufficient characterization, and the result is superficiality—and rejection letters.

Who are these people in nonfiction? They are the people you interview, quote, and describe: the husband-wife owners of the spa in your consumer service piece; the gas station attendant who, in your feature, dove into the river and saved the child. Finally, *you* are the character in your first-person essay about what it was like to be the victim of identity theft.

Characterization occurs by levels, and not all levels are appropriate for every piece of writing. Your best guide is to read examples of writing similar to yours. You can also build your understanding of characterization in nonfiction by reading books on craft for novelists, such as *Dynamic Characters*, by Nancy Kress, and *45 Master Characters*, by Victoria Lynn Schmidt.

Characterization of yourself as narrator and others occurs through the following elements: facts, physical description, actions, first impressions, interpretations of motivation and psychology, exposition (summary of past events), accomplishments, anecdotes, metaphors, opinions and biases, speech tags and mannerisms, and other people's descriptions, reports, and impressions.

One of the biggest problems in writing about yourself is revealing to the reader what seems so obvious to you. Invariably, writers believe they are "sharing all," when they are actually revealing little of what is important. One of the best ways to correct this problem is to ask yourself every few paragraphs, "What am I feeling now?" "What is my emotional truth at this point in sharing my life experience?" As you recount the incidents in your story, you should be revealing the changes in your emotions. If you have no emotions on a page—a common weakness—then the reader can only relate to you intellectually. They are unlikely to identify your yearning, your story promise, and they will feel as if you created a barrier on purpose. None of us likes to be walled out.

DRAMATIC STRUCTURE

From Aristotle, we get the three parts of dramatic structure: problem, conflict, resolution. This simple sequence underlies the three-act play and the evolution of the novel. As modern storytellers, we have the advantage of using the twelve-step Hero's Journey delineated by the late mythologist Joseph Campbell (see Map 8-2 in North). This quest form offers a particularly apt blueprint for writing about people in book length.

The most common problem with autobiographical writing is an absence of dramatic structure and an overabundance of episodic structure. Autobiographical writing—personal experience, memoir, or autobiography—often suffers from episodic structure. Episodes appear strung together, like beads on a line, until the writer decides, seemingly arbitrarily, to end. Episodic structure rarely satisfies any reader who does not personally know the writer. Why? Episodic writing lacks an "arc." One incident seems identical to the prior in intensity and meaning.

In contrast, dramatic structure foretells the conclusion by identifying what's being sought and what's at stake from the beginning of the story. Dramatic structure creates a crescendo of suspense. Readers always know where they are relative to the beginning, the struggle, and the climax. They can invest in the outcome. The series of incidents in episodic writing creates a flat line. No suspense. And for the writer—plenty of rejections.

SCENE STRUCTURE

Related to the overall dramatic structure is the smaller unit of scene structure. Double-check your people stories to make sure you have all the elements of a strong scene: a clear-cut goal at the top of the scene; details of opposition; interior reflection; formulation of new strategies by your narrator to reach the goal; repetition of opposition and obstacles; and finally, success. This resolution should be accompanied by something unexpected. Success may be bittersweet; there may be a price. In the last scene, show your narrator's realization of a thematic truth.

DESCRIPTION

Another weakness in stories about people is too much "telling" and not enough "showing." *Telling* refers to a reporter-like description of events, also referred to as narration. *Showing* refers to the creation of scenes, like a reenactment with dialogue, action, description of people and setting, and expression of the sensory experience of the narrator. Use the balance of telling and showing that best matches your kind of writing.

DEPTH AND AUTHENTICITY

An essay or memoir may display beautiful and original writing. It may be technically and structurally sound. If the piece is read to a critique group, it will surely receive accolades. But in the deep silence that follows, everyone will be searching for words to express a "feeling" that something isn't quite right. What's wrong?

In my experience, these pieces usually lack soul. The writing is inauthentic if it doesn't evoke the author's truth. It is equally possible that the author doesn't know what that truth is. The inner process to find one's truth and express it fully means "soul" searching. Often, uncomfortable emotions, threshold guardians (any outer distraction that would keep us from our quest), and a host of habitual defense mechanisms arise to prevent some writers from seeing the unvarnished emotional truths.

To troubleshoot problems with depth and authenticity, read your work to yourself while asking such questions as: "What did I feel at this moment?" "What deeper issue or concern did this action trigger?" "What suffering was I feeling at this point in my experience?"

One of the mistakes in typical approaches to writing is the assumption that once a writer decides on a theme, his job is done. You won't communicate an emotional honesty about your work if you approach it intellectually. Authenticity has passion borne of suffering and joy. The writer's interaction with his inner truth and the written word is a process that continues word by word—or "bird by bird" as Anne Lamott has said in her book whose title uses the same phrase.

Writing About Ideas

A Chinese proverb captures the central problem that besets essays about ideas: "With reason one can travel the world over; without it, it is hard to move an inch."

We have a rich philosophical heritage underlying the exploration of ideas. It rests on the foundation of reason. I doubt that our schools include, or emphasize, how to cultivate the reasoning capacity. I wish I had more training myself. The study of mathematics helps, as does any formal study of logic in philosophy.

Clearly, if you have chosen to write about an idea, you must *feel passionately* about it, which will seem contradictory to the emphasis on reason. The ideal might be "reasoned passion." To care deeply is a virtue, and if you want to communicate, even transfer, that caring to your reader, double-check the logical underpinnings of your writing.

A good place to begin self-diagnosis is with the broad categories of ideas. As we discussed in chapter nine, decide whether you are discussing philosophy, metaphysics, aesthetics, or ethics. That way, you can begin with a clear head knowing that your writing explores ideas related to taste, morality, or the Big Ideas—the nature of being, the origin and structure of the world, or a theory of knowledge.

Without this clear knowledge, I can almost guarantee that your presentation will have lapses in logical consistency or places where passion replaces the next step in a sound argument instead of merely "informing" it.

Read your newspaper's letters to the editor. You'll quickly see that most of them offer an opinion of taste or morality. However, after these authors give their opinions, the rest of their letters fail to offer support; instead they entertain (or irritate) with tirades and personality but little to persuade the reader to their viewpoints.

The foundation of effective writing about ideas, where your intent is to persuade, is classic argument structure. Identify your audience, or you could insult the reader's intelligence or confuse him with unfamiliar details. State your proposition—what you are trying to prove—in one sentence, for yourself first, and then for your reader. Define your terms, especially ones that are critical to the particular idea under discussion. Don't make assumptions.

One common problem in idea pieces that have otherwise been well set up is a mismatch of claims and support. Suppose you wanted to write about your wish to turn a dead downtown into a thriving cultural and artistic center, something I've long thought my city, Eugene, Oregon, should do. If this argument made a claim of policy—the voters or city council should pass a law—the argument would be weaker than a claim of value—a thriving cultural and artistic center would enhance Eugene's aesthetic reputation.

An argument can be weakened with a wrong choice of support as well. In the above example, I could infer that political corruption blocks this fine idea, and I could toss out names and past events as my support. Sour grapes! Perhaps a motivational appeal would be sounder, but perhaps not. Hard evidence could be the best match. How do you decide what's your best support in an argument? Go back; for whom have you gone to all of this trouble? Your readers. Decisions about claims and support depend on your audience over all other considerations. Last of all, consider how strong your warrant is as a measure for choosing both the claim and support. Keep the strength of warrant in mind as you work to improve all of your writing about ideas.

If your primary intent is to inform, then your exploration of ideas may not follow the classical argument structure. You may be writing in any of the major fields of study: education, business, science, psychology, history, and others. Check your writing for the following common problems: logical progression of topics and subtopics according to your chosen method of organization, parallel development (meaning similar detail, in development and examples, of topics and subtopics), definitions of terms, and specificity—of facts, figures, examples, cases, studies, and quoted authorities.

Writing About Things

Writing about information related to things, news about things, and how to deal with things consumes an enormous quantity of the market. Your writing can shipwreck on the rocks for reasons already addressed: problems with conception and problems with structure. But it can also break into smithereens for other reasons.

SCOPE AND "DPI"

A common problem is scope. One of my students had an idea for a book on parenting. When she told me her working subtitle, *From Infancy Through Teens,* I knew right away she was in trouble. I explained to her that parents are highly interested in help with raising their children at each age or grade. If their kids are preschoolers, however, they're unlikely to pay for a book where half of it covers issues of teen sex, drug use, and emotions gone haywire. Her scope was too wide.

Other times, the writer has set the parameters for the subject too narrowly for an intended market. For instance, I once had a client who wanted to write a book about her city's conflict between the environmentalists and the developers and how the resolution changed both groups. On the one hand, this issue is universal; it affects most towns and cities in the United States, Canada, and elsewhere.

The writer and I talked about the chances of her story, as a book, getting picked up by a large publisher with wide distribution. As I saw it, she was unlikely to gain reader interest beyond her state, even though she had an important difference to make related to this issue. The specificity of the story—names of people, companies, politicians, developments, local and state laws—made the book seem too narrow. Even while I formed this opinion, another voice cautioned me that if her writing were outstanding enough, her story could transcend the limited scope and even win awards for her investigative journalism.

All writers of information articles about things face the fine line between a narrow—and salable—scope and a scope *too* narrow for their market. Scientists and people in technical professions in particular face this problem. The life cycle of a flea or the application software of the UX-469AG-3591 may elicit high interest but only from a few readers.

You can end up with far too much material and err by trying to cram it all into your article or book. Because writers become experts by virtue of their research, if they are not already experts on a subject by vocation, they may not recognize that their readers can't absorb so much.

One of my editing clients is a former professor of art history who has had one textbook published. She decided to share her love of history by writing another book for the general public. I created a new measurement for the only major problem in her material: "dpi." Density per inch. Even with my background in humanities and a master's degree, I couldn't keep up with the dpi. Her vocabulary matched the reading public's level and her style was entertaining with a killer wry humor. She simply introduced too much material in too little a space. Fortunately, with an IQ in the stratosphere and the determination of an Olympic athlete, she listened, she revised, and she now has a literary agent.

Although this professor's problem was due to having too much of a good thing, other writers struggle with too little substance.

We've all read articles and books that are primarily "fluff." The dpi rating is too low. Generalities frequently accompany a low density of substance. Sweeping statements of truth without support usually mean that the author has done too little research, and the material has insufficient factual basis.

CLEAR INSTRUCTIONS

Problems related to clarity afflict writing across the board. When there is a problem with clarity in a how-to article or book, the effect can be disastrous. How frustrating for a reader to follow each step in a set of instructions only to get stuck with a muddled one that stops completion cold!

When you write instructions for how to write a how-to book or how to construct a gazebo for your garden, you *must* read your instructions aloud. Mentally retrace your steps or ask a friend to follow your directions and build that gazebo. Revise as needed.

A particular kind of how-to instruction, the food-recipe article and the cookbook, require careful replication of instructions. You probably cook by instincts and intuition if you have spent years devoted to the culinary arts. Warning: novice readers will take *every word* literally. I often think of a man I once dated who, newly divorced after a twenty-year marriage, proudly told me that he'd just learned how to boil water—and I'm not making this up! Make sure your instructions leave nothing out.

REVIEWS

Reviewing books, movies, plays, concerts, and any of the arts is a specialty area in writing about things. An aura of glamour and power surround the reviewer. Siskel and Ebert, before Siskel died, became cultural icons, celebrities in their own right, and they made reviewing movies look so easy.

If you decide to become a reviewer, you'll need to blend forms: in-depth analysis with argument. You'll use the tools of aesthetics to write about things. Sometimes, you'll draw from ethics and even metaphysics to provide the depth and perspective your subject needs.

Many writers feel drawn to becoming reviewers, but you'll run into problems if you're not steeped in the subject. "Everyone is entitled to an opinion," goes the saying, but a reviewer's opinion should be schooled. Otherwise, you'll be unable to draw comparisons between one movie and another, to place a current work in the history of an author's career, or to recommend one recording over another for a symphony.

Assuming that you have a specialized background to write reviews for your chosen art, you could still draw a hail of tomatoes from your readers if you "go technical" on them. The role of the reviewer is as translator for readers. You stand between the scholar and the interested layperson. I've long admired how wine reviewers put into words something as difficult to describe as a taste. Music reviewers, likewise, must describe sounds. How does one describe an ineffable yet palpable tenderness expressed by the viola in the last held note?

A reviewer's job is not to annihilate their subject; nor is it to sugarcoat reality. Be overly critical, and you probably won't keep your job. Be not critical enough, and you probably won't keep your job. Read reviews written by the best in your field. One way that reviewers handle this delicate balance is by complimenting what is done well at the beginning of the review and then, often three-quarters through, shifting to criticism. Instead of making sweeping statements—almost never a good idea—they offer specific criticism and end the review with a personal evaluation.

NEWS

A substantial portion of information writing is reporting. Even when you have done successful troubleshooting of your structure—from lead to conclusion—and have subjected your writing to the rigors of copyediting, problems may undercut success.

The quality of your information based on the quality of your sources determines the viability of your writing. One source is people, and they vary in "quality" based on their expertise, reputation,

RECOMMENDED BOOKS ON HOW TO INTERVIEW

Creative Interviewing: The Writer's Guide to Gathering Information by Asking Questions by Ken Metzler

Interviewing America's Top Interviewers: 19 Top Interviewers Tell All About What They Do by Jack T. Huber and Dean Diggins

Interviewing: Art and Skill by Jeanne Tessier Barone and Jo Young Switzer

and celebrity. However, you can interview the president of the United States and come away with a useless set of information, and not just because he—or she (hope springs eternal)—is a politician.

Interviewing is an art and a skill. You have to ask the right questions in the right way to find the "real" story and to get the direct quotes that will illuminate it. How to interview is beyond the scope of this book. However, there are many fine books on the subject, some of which are listed in the resource box.

Books, magazines, journals, newspapers, and Internet sites all provide source materials. As you may remember from research methods in school, there are two types of sources—primary and secondary. Primary resources are better because your information originates directly from the source of the knowledge. In the vernacular, you've received your information from the horse's mouth and not second-hand.

You should trace your secondary sources back to a primary source for one obvious reason: accuracy. Inaccuracy weakens all parts of an article, essay, or book, even if only one fact, quotation, or explanation is inaccurate.

Writing About Places

If you write about travel, nature, or the outdoors as how-to or information writing, then you are most likely to encounter problems with structure, accuracy of information, and specificity. To troubleshoot these kinds of problems, refer to the other sections in South and also to the chapters on writing about things. If the emphasis in your writing about place is on people, review the sections here and in the chapters on writing about people.

Two extremely difficult problems to correct in writing about places in travel narratives and travel memoirs are weak author voice and lack of verisimilitude of place.

AUTHOR VOICE

What is *Voice*? A simple definition is the unique way that a writer combines the story elements. A more complex definition is this: *Voice* refers to the style, diction, and even content that when expressed through the writer's perceptions and sensibilities creates for the reader a sense of communicating with an individual unlike any other. Editors and agents simply say, "fresh and original."

Like the other forms of personal-experience writing, travel narratives are highly demanding of the writer to find original ways of seeing a landscape and its people and to find fresh expressions for both inner and outer experiences. The worst voice for writing about places, in my opinion, is the chamber-of-commerce voice, a mixture of canned superlatives and advertising hype.

So how do you cultivate an original voice? First, you must master your control over the basic elements of writing. This might seem obvious and perhaps superfluous, but writing well takes practice. Writing with originality is built upon the foundation of writing well. I recommend studying (not just reading) William Zinsser's classic, *On Writing Well.* Also study *Make Your Words Work,* by Gary Provost. And, read poetry, some of the most original writing we have.

Read. Read travel, nature, and outdoor writing. Read critically. This involves paying attention to how various writers use language to achieve what effects. If you really want to internalize how an author you admire writes, take the time to type his or her essay or chapter—word for word. You'll get a body experience that is different from your mental observations. A next step is to emulate an author's style. Choose one paragraph, for instance, and write your own using that author's sentence structure, diction, tone, and imagery.

Most of all, you want to discover and cultivate your own voice that is unlike any other person's on the planet. After you finish a rough draft, don't allow yourself to be satisfied with any paragraph that, when lifted from your writing, could be attributed to anyone. How do you do this? I think of this part of the process as "harvesting." Read your work to yourself slowly, paying attention to your inner feelings, memories, and images. Read slowly enough that you can harvest them and work them into your writing. Go overboard to begin with. Overwrite. You can trim back later. Most writers underwrite, failing to develop their perceptions, emotions, memories, and visual images.

VERISIMILITUDE

This great word that massages the tongue means creating a sensation for the reader that the world on paper is real. It's about creating the appearance of reality. Writing about places is nothing if it does not have verisimilitude. The best travel, nature, and outdoor writing transports the reader to the place and, coupled with the author's voice, gives the reader a vicarious experience.

How do you accomplish this seemingly formidable task? Some of the task is dependent upon your ability to "see." Two people can stand in the same spot and one can find nothing to appreciate while the other could write a book on it.

A second aspect of giving the appearance of reality is expanding your knowledge of the place you're writing about. That's why research is a key component of writing about place. You won't go wrong by becoming a lay expert in geology, geography, anthropology, archaeology, the environmental sciences, and, for urban locations, history, popular culture, art and architecture, and languages. I'm sure the list could grow. The direct result of studying broadly related to a place you want to write about is an increase in details. *Travel Writing in Fiction and Fact,* by Jane Edwards, will help you teach yourself to do this, and it will improve your writer's voice. When I hike in the Cascades in Oregon, for instance, I typically notice only the plants and flowers that I can name. The more you know, the more you can appreciate and write about.

As in cultivating your original voice, you can increase your skill in verisimilitude by reading how other writers have depicted the same places you write about and by emulating them. Just about everywhere has been written about, which is why writing about places has such a high demand for originality.

To build your skill in voice and verisimilitude, try keeping a journal of observations, images, and sensations. *Keeping a Nature Journal: Discover a Whole New Way of Seeing the World Around You*, by Clare Walker Leslie and Charles E. Roth, is a resource that may guide you in this practice. Most writers rely on their visual sense to the exclusion of others. Open those doors of perception to sound, smell, taste, temperature, angle of the sun, wind, rain, snow, dust, dirt, sand, altitude, and other experiences, and find ways to describe them that are all your own.

EAST

Your Rising Star

THIRTEEN

Learning How to Market

Of course I realized there was a measure of danger. Obviously I faced the possibility of not returning when I first considered going. Once faced and settled there really wasn't any good reason to refer to it again.

Amelia Earhart

WRITING IS A COMMUNICATION art. Marketing is a communication science. What do I mean by this? Once you've reached your destination—you have a completed article, essay, or book—seeing it published is mostly mechanical. The hardest, most creative part is over.

If you've done any marketing and have rejection letters to show for it, you may disagree. However, editors of all kinds of publications, and literary agents who represent book manuscripts, repeatedly identify two reasons that account for 99 percent of all rejections. Number one, the writing is not ready to publish. Number two, the manuscript was sent to the wrong place.

Increasing your skill over time will overcome the first problem of unpolished or amateurish writing. Assuming that you use this book to guide you in writing well-constructed articles, essays, and books, with practice you'll produce writing worthy of publication. Further, if in tandem you develop self-editing skills like those outlined in chapter twelve, you'll minimize rejection. Because none of us can see our own work objectively—not even professional writers, most writers rely on critique groups, friends, and freelance editors to provide feedback and constructive criticism.

Finding a remedy for the second problem, manuscripts sent to the wrong place, involves entirely different skills than writing. Because this problem is routinely reported by editors and agents as a big one, that can only mean two possibilities: writers by the thousands and hundreds of thousands have not done their homework, or writers have not learned how to market. Knowing where to send your manuscripts and how to approach editors and agents is not rocket science; it can be learned.

Far too many writers have been using the note-in-the-bottle approach to marketing. They put their manuscript—the note—in an envelope or box—the bottle—and cast it into the sea, a decision both nondiscriminating and foolish. These writers wait to get a positive response that never comes.

If not rocket science, how can a writer nevertheless turn marketing into a predictable science with predictable results? Assuming your writing is ready to be published, successful marketing involves four steps:

- Attitude
- Research
- Sales
- Results

Attitude

Success in everything comes down to attitude; isn't that all too true? When I sat on a panel of authors who were asked to address marketing, the other two authors spoke first, offering terrific suggestions for getting publicity. Then it was my turn to speak. I surveyed the audience of about sixty people and asked a question I knew was a trap.

"How many of you find marketing not only to be unpleasant, but to rank right up there with taking old fish out to the garbage?"

As I expected, about fifty-five hands shot up.

"That's your problem," I said. "You've got to change your attitude."

If you find anything unpleasant, you're going to do it poorly, or at least you'll post blocks to doing it well. Selling is not a writer's devil. We are not selling our souls. We simply want to share our ideas and stories with other people to whom we hope to make a difference. What's not to admire about that?

The truth is that marketing is a people business. We communicate with editors or agents and seek their acceptance of our work. Editors and agents need what writers have to offer. They don't take glee in rejecting writers. In fact, that is one of the unpleasant parts of their job. If writers realize that everyone holds the same goal—supplying the public with writing they appreciate, it would make everyone's job easier.

> **Marketing is a people business. Editors and agents need what writers have to offer.**

Too many rejections in a marketplace that is highly competitive and bottom-line driven can sour even the positive thinkers. Because we are still making the transition into the new era of making differences, the old era's thinking—*how* can we make money, more money, and more money—still dominates. This mentality in corporate publishing is a far cry from *what difference* this piece of writing makes in our readers' lives. In the new era, and among some publishers even now, one question will be, "Is our publishing company's vision aligned with the writer's vision?"

The best attitude to adopt for marketing is to consider it as yet another adventure, as another wilderness through which you intend to find a path. If you approach the task as an explorer, expecting to encounter difficulties and unexpected rewards, you'll adopt the best attitude for success.

Research

Once again, you need a clear map. In this case, the map for marketing success includes directories of publications and postings of their writer's guidelines. The listings in directories outline the specifications for writing that publications seek. You could consider these listings as their want-ads—"General interest magazine in search of a compatible article."

Bookstores and libraries carry directories, but you need to know which ones match your needs. Some of the most common directories include:

- *The Writer's Handbook* and *Writer's Market*: includes markets for articles, essays, and books.

- *Children's Writer's & Illustrator's Market*: specializes in publications targeted at youths.

- *Directory of Literary Magazines*: features publications seeking articles, essays, and short stories.

- *Literary Market Place*: the bible of the book publishing industry that lists publishers both large and small and literary agents—not a directory of magazine or newspaper markets.

- *Guide to Literary Agents*: updated annually by Writer's Digest Publications, this guide lists over 600 agents, including a section on script agents. The guide includes membership in the Association of Authors' Representatives (AAR), it lists how long an agent has been in business, and it states their preferences for queries and submission—and much more.

- *Writer's Guide to Book Editors, Publishers, and Literary Agents*: written by literary agent Jeff Herman and his staff, this directory is updated every two years. As indicated in the title, this guide profiles book publishers and is unique by listing in-house editors, information not listed in other directories. The profile of about 300 agents includes more personal data than other directories in an effort to help writers find simpatico matches.

Nowadays, writers must develop the skill of using the Internet. It has become as fundamental to our work as the word processing function of our computers. If you are not yet facile with surfing the web, then a librarian can help you. Every publication has a web site where they post their writer's guidelines. Most literary agents now have web sites (and if you are writing a book for which you are seeking representation, you're generally expected to have or develop a web site, too). Even though these web sites are invaluable for market research, I still like having a paper directory where I can quickly thumb through listings, make notations, and return quickly for reference. Call me paper dependent.

Every directory includes instructions in the beginning for how to use it and to decipher the language of the specifications. For instance, here are some of the terms, and their meanings, that you must learn:

- Circulation—how many subscribers

- AAR—Association of Authors' Representatives. It's preferable to have your agent belong because of membership requirements to sell at least twelve books a year and to adhere to the AAR code of ethics and guidelines for financial practices.

- RWA—Romance Writers of America

- Query—the letter you send to present your idea or work

- Clips—photocopies of published pieces of your writing

- Multiple submissions—will consider your manuscript if you have sent it to many places at the same time

- Exclusive submissions—will consider your manuscript only if you refrain from sending it elsewhere at the same time

- Kill fee—amount of money paid if the magazine decides not to use your piece after they have contracted for it

- Advance—a portion of future book royalties paid ahead of publication

- Royalties—a percentage of the retail—or wholesale—price of a book that is the author's payment

You'll also see terminology that should be familiar after reading this book, terms that identify the different forms of writing.

Your job involves culling through directories and guidelines to determine the best places to send your manuscript. The key word is "best." What is a best place?

A best market for your writing is one that matches your subject, style, and slant with a particular publication's subject, style, and slant. A best market reaches your targeted reader. A best market offers you conditions of publication that you find acceptable, conditions such as response time, payment, and prestige.

If you are marketing a book, you may be seeking a literary agent who in turn will find the best publisher for your work. If so, you may wonder what constitutes a "best" agent. Similar criteria apply: you want an agent who has a track record selling your kind of subject matter and genre. Because an agent takes over the job of selling, you also want someone who has proven sales skill, and nothing documents this better than a list of published titles and authors. You also want someone who upholds ethical standards and accounting practices. Membership in the AAR is one guarantee of this requirement. Last of all, and not least of all, you want an agent with personal integrity and with whom you can communicate—as often and as well as you need.

But do you need a literary agent to find a publisher for your book? Upward of 90 percent of all books published each year have been agent represented, and many of the large publishers seldom consider queries or book proposals from unagented writers. That said, not all books meet the requirements—by subject, size of au-

WEB SITES FOR FINDING MARKETS

www.writing-world.com

www.zinebook.com

www.worldwidefreelance.com

www.writers.net

www.suite101.com

www.ewritersplace.com

www.refdesk.com

www.spannet.org

www.pilot-search.com

www.publist.com

www.amazon.com

www.google.com

www.ebooknet.com

www.aar-online.org

www.bookwire.com

www.abe.com

dience, or scope—of large publishers, and therefore of the agents who sell to them. There are literally hundreds of midsized, small, regional, university, and specialty publishers that prefer submissions directly from writers. You've got to do your homework to make the right match.

> **A best market is one that matches your subject, style, and slant, while meeting your needs for response time, payment, and prestige.**

Directories and web sites are two places to learn where you can find a home for your manuscripts. However, you can rarely beat a personal referral or recommendation. "I'd like to introduce you to my friend, the regional editor for *Love* magazine," will facilitate marketing an article idea better than a cold query to the same person at the same magazine. Remember, marketing is a people business first. Cultivate connections with writers, teachers, editors, agents, and anyone else related to publishing.

When writers begin to market their works, they often have unrealistic ideas about the quality of their writing and the markets that would be interested in publishing them. The saying "paying one's dues" comes to mind. Even if your writing matches the quality of the most prestigious magazines, unless you have clips—those photocopies of your prior published works—in similar markets, you may be passed over.

Want to see a bunch of writers howl with laughter? Ask them to share their first experiences of marketing, including where they sent their manuscripts or queries. Be prepared to hear a list of the most outstanding magazines in this country: *The Atlantic Monthly, Harper's, The New Yorker, Playboy, Gentleman's Quarterly,* as well as the top-circulation women's magazines. "I've been rejected by the best," one of my friends quips. Another friend shows his prized scrapbook of rejection letters typed on some of the most hoity-toity stationery in the country.

Another mistake of beginning marketers is making a short list, instead of a long list, of places that might publish their works. The problem with selecting only a few possibilities is that once these publications (or agents) reject a writer, he or she often fails to pursue other options.

The science of marketing means that a systematic approach pays off. I recommend selecting a dozen places or people *at the same time*. In other words, you may very well have to market to a first dozen, a second dozen, a third dozen, and so forth, before a given piece of writing finds its home.

Your research should help you select the very best, and most realistic, options. If you want to include some high-end possibilities, I won't dissuade you. There is something to be said for aiming high and finding your entry level based on trial and error. I have also watched wonderful writers who aimed too low, never approaching higher-circulation or more prestigious publications. Each writer must define her comfort zone and expectations.

In my opinion, the best choice is neither choosing the top markets and working down or choosing the low markets and working up. Instead, nothing beats knowing a magazine or journal so well, for instance, that you know if your subject, writing, and slant match its identity. Chances are, your selection of a dozen possible markets will include some publications with which you are well acquainted and to which you may even be a subscriber. If you pursue a systematic approach, you will browse three to six issues of every magazine on your list of prospects.

By "browse," I don't mean the casual way you might read magazines in a doctor's office. I'm talking about "intentional browsing" to pick up key factors that define the publication. What are these key factors? Some of these factors include:

- the depth and breadth of the subject matter

- analysis of the level of diction, such as formal or informal, chatty or scholarly

- the political and social leaning and any other demographic factors

- the average length of the articles or essays

- a determination of how many pieces are staff written versus freelance written

- the frequency of examples, anecdotes, and quoted authorities

- the density of statistics and facts

Look at the ads. Advertisers will not throw away money. They know who reads the magazine and buys the products they sell. They identify reader needs and use models in the ads that reflect the reader demographics. You can contact the publication and ask for an advertising packet that includes a profile of the readership. This gives you very specific information about who their reader—your audience—is.

You'll discover how different it is to examine a publication as a writer looking for a market rather than as a reader seeking information or entertainment. To critically examine a number of issues takes time and effort, but your prospect list will be more accurate. You won't waste your time and that of editors by mailing queries and manuscripts to an inappropriate market.

Pick a dozen potential markets (or literary agents). There is actually a label for doing this: "The Rule of Twelve." Rank your twelve selections in order of preference and realistic possibility of success. *If* your number one choice has the bad taste to reject your manuscript, you know precisely where to send it next. You look at your list and send it to number two. Moreover, if you establish a routine of responding to a rejection letter by immediately mailing out your query or manuscript to the next selection on your list, you'll increase your odds of success and decrease the temptation to sabotage your marketing efforts by not taking further action.

Sales

Once you know the best "outlets" for your writing, you're ready to make your sales presentation, which comes in many different styles. If you have a chance to meet with an editor or agent, you can make a verbal sales pitch. If your article or essay is short, under 1,000 words, or if the directory tells you to send the completed manuscript, your sales document is the cover letter. If your work is longer than 1,000 words or if you are marketing a book, the query letter is your first step in making a sale. Because most editors and agents get hundreds of solicitations each week, and reject most of them, everything rides on the query letter. If you plan to market a book, you'll also need to write a proposal, which makes the sales pitch to publishers that you or your agent query. Let's briefly cover each one of these four vehicles of sales:

- Verbal pitch
- Cover letter
- Query letter
- Proposal

VERBAL PITCH

Most of us don't rub shoulders with agents and editors in our social circles, so writers' conferences are the place where you will have a chance to meet these professionals. If you don't already know what conferences meet in your region, go to a web site that lists almost all conferences—worldwide: www.shawguides.com. Many of the conferences and workshops include one-on-one or group appointments with the guest agents and editors. Even if this is not a feature, you can always *make* an opportunity to speak with an agent or editor—after a panel, in an elevator, while talking with other writers during breaks. They universally agree on where they don't want to hear a pitch: in the rest room. If you think I'm joking, go to a large conference and follow an agent into the rest room and watch and listen to the other people there—or maybe only women talk in such circumstances.

Your verbal pitch should be the proverbial twenty-five words or less. You'll be hard-pressed to memorize more than this amount anyway. More to the point, beyond twenty-five words and you'll begin to ramble away from describing the essential information about your project. One of my published editing clients said that he believes all writers should seek training in business communications and acting. Certainly, both come in handy for succeeding at the verbal pitch. An agent I know, Tom Grady, suggested that writers fill in the blank: Next on *Oprah*, _____. How would you describe your nonfiction book, or article, or memoir if one of the new book-club hosts gave you a call and asked you, "So, what's it about?"

When it comes to pitching your ideas in the written forms of a cover letter, query letter, or book proposal, there are rules for format, paper quality, and mailing. Independent of how well you've written your letters, if you stumble on these conventions, no one may even bother to read further. Many directories, such as *Writer's Market*, outline these rules. Consult Map 13-2 before you print and mail.

COVER LETTER

A cover letter sent with a manuscript is a business formality, a courtesy, and an opportunity. For one thing, it contains vital information for the routing clerks: author contact information, editor, date of letter, and title of work. But it can be much more.

A cover letter is a showcase of your writing and your attitude. If it is clean, printed with dark ink on nice paper, perhaps on an attractive letterhead, then the writer has already communicated something vital to the editor. The writer has said, "I care. I am a professional. I understand first impressions, and I want to impress you."

A cover letter can rekindle a prior connection by reminding the editor of a request for the manuscript. For instance, if a friend has referred you, or if the editor you met at a conference has invited you to send your manuscript, remind him of this fact in your first line. If there has not been a prior request, then your letter should indicate that you are enclosing "the article per guidelines in *The Writer's Handbook*" or other source.

Cover letters are short. You should get down to business and state what you're enclosing, its length, and its working title. "The enclosed humor piece, 'A Day in the Life of Ivan Voinovich Petoulie Oil,' is 750 words long."

What turns a cover letter into a sales presentation is the addition of two more items: (1) a sentence or two about the theme, promise, or slant of your enclosed article or story, and (2) a paragraph about you that lists any publishing credits or any other relevant information about you. For example, a paragraph about the theme of your piece might look like this: "My Mother's Day feature explores the love of unwed teen mothers for their babies. As a health-care professional working with these young mothers, I have witnessed the transformative power of their love. I have written this piece with hope that the article will bring more acceptance and assistance to these unsung, beautiful young women and their babies."

In your last paragraph, list any publishing credits that seem appropriate for the manuscript you have enclosed and for the stature of the publication. In other words, omit mention of your articles "published" in the church newsletter if you hope to sell your article to *Working Mother.* However, if you are a frequent contributing writer to an e-zine for professional women, or for working mothers, you should mention these credentials specifically.

Don't worry if you have no publications to tout because you are just beginning to market your work. You still have author data to provide. If you have any personal reason for writing the manuscript you've enclosed, say so, but limit yourself to a sentence or two. In the end, if you can think of nothing to say, you can at least add, "I am a freelance writer and have read and enjoyed your magazine for years." Last of all, always but always enclose a self-addressed stamped envelope (SASE).

QUERY LETTER

A query letter solicits an agent or editor's interest in your idea or manuscript. When a directory tells you to "query first," do not send your manuscript. One of my literary agent friends told me that she uses her "query only" guideline as a first test of how well she can work with a client. "If they can't follow directions," she said, "then I know they will not be easy to work with."

Like all forms of nonfiction, the query has a lead, body, and conclusion. Select one of the fifteen types of leads mentioned in chapter five and introduce your article, essay, or book. Here's an example of a narrative or descriptive lead written by freelancer,

Mabel Armstrong, in her successful query letter to *Faces: People, Places, and Cultures,* a magazine for children published by Cobblestone Publishing Company:

> Living in a little village at the northern tip of Andros Island in the Bahamas are the remains of a band of escaped slaves. They are descendants of African slaves who fled from the southern states into Florida, where they lived among the native Seminoles. During the Spanish American War, a small group of those escaped slaves, now called Black Seminoles, made their way across the Atlantic to Andros Island, and settled at Red Bays. Here they produce unique baskets made of palm fronds.

Follow the lead with a clear statement of your purpose and the kind of manuscript you wish to send. Here is the continuation of the query by Mabel Armstrong:

> In my 400-word article, "The Basket Sewers of Red Bays," I will focus on a family at Red Bays as they harvest palm fronds, process them, and make baskets, a process they call "sewing."

Your statement about the subject may describe the manuscript's length, audience, theme, or other details. For example: "My memoir is 85,000 words. Written from the heart, I want to offer hope to other parents whose teenager has suffered serious mental illness." Or, "I propose a consumer-product piece, about 750 words, that is a roundup of the best ergonomic keyboards."

In the body of your query, use the facts, statistics, and quoted remarks from authorities related to your subject. By doing this, you fill out the background on your manuscript, show that you have done preliminary research, and build a case for reader interest in your ideas. Basically, you need to convince the agent or editor that your subject is timely, relevant, and meets the needs of the reader. Because each publication has a definite audience, identity, and slant, your query should reflect your understanding of the publication's needs and communicate your professionalism.

If your query letter proposes an article, the body tells how you

You need to convince the agent or editor that your subject is timely, relevant, and meets the needs of the reader.

intend to develop the manuscript, structurally and in terms of content. Will you interview anyone? Tell whom you intend to contact and why. What method of organization will you use? You may state this and impress the editor that you know how to organize your writing. For example, "Developed in ascending order of complexity, my technical article begins with definitions and simple concepts of . . ."

In Mabel Armstrong's query for the article "The Basket Sewers of Red Bays," she submitted an outline for her article as requested in the writer's guidelines of the publication. She used the body of her query instead to let the editor know about the sidebar and photos she intended to include. She also listed her sources for the article, again per the writer's guidelines.

Readers can also learn, in a sidebar, how to make a cooling drink with tamarind, a native plant used for flavorings as well as for beverages. I can provide photos of the baskets, Andros Island, and Red Bays.

My sources for the article include: *The Seminoles of Florida,* James W. Covington, University Press of Florida, 1993; *The Black Seminoles,* Kenneth W. Porter, University Press of Florida, 1996; *West Indies,* Philip Sherlock, Walker and Co., New York, 1966; and *Baskets of Southeastern Indians,* R. Gettys, Ethnographic Arts Publications, 1984.

The body of a query for a nonfiction book has more development than a body for an article. The writer often mentions competitive books and compares her book, emphasizing how her proposed book is unique and possibly better than ones already on the market. The body may describe the audience for the book and offer statistics that define the size—mass, substantial, specialized/small—of the primary audience. A query for a book should also emphasize the benefit to the reader and describe special features of the proposed book.

The last part of the body of the query, whether for an article, essay, or book, offers the writer's credits and some biographical detail. In this one paragraph, the writer lists prior publishing successes and any personal or professional background relevant to the proposed work.

The conclusion seeks to close the sale. Always upbeat, the writer suggests that the agent or editor request the manuscript. In other words, you should never sound doubtful or beg. For a book, you might write, "I have a completed book proposal that includes sixty pages of sample chapters that I would be happy to send upon your request." For an article, you might write, "I plan to interview Dr. X and Dr. Y within two weeks, and I see my proposed article as an ideal for a tie-in with the spring pollen season. I look forward to hearing from you at your earliest convenience." For an essay, you might write, "My positive experiences of traveling as a woman alone in the Middle East last summer seem like a good match for your summer issue. I look forward to hearing from you. . . ."

Query length has shrunk over the years. Strive to keep your queries to one page, even if it means you need to make your letterhead smaller or redesign it. Of course, there are always exceptions. Map 13-1 at chapter's end provides a longer query that nonetheless brought a go-ahead by the publication and then a sale. Queries for nonfiction books may exceed the one-page rule because they are expected to offer more information.

Writing a successful query that defies the high rate of rejection is an art and a skill. They take practice like any other form of writing. You'll know you've arrived when you no longer have to write queries. Instead, you'll pick up the phone, call *your* editor or agent and discuss your idea for a next article, essay, or book.

PROPOSAL

Proposals take two forms—proposals for articles and proposals for books.

Proposals for Articles

The article proposal typically includes an outline of the proposed article, something not included in a query. If you do not have a proven record of success or if you are querying on a complex topic, an article proposal, by its detail, offers security to the editor. Typically several pages in length, if it includes a developed outline of your piece, the article proposal allows the editor to make suggestions before you complete your research, do interviews, or write the article. Chapter six in North should help you get your bearings and construct a solid outline. The article proposal also gives the writer a good feeling of security. You nail down what you are going to write and how you're going to do it.

Book Proposals

Book proposals are complex documents, as well they should be, since they are the sales presentation for which authors receive five- and six-figure dollar amounts and sometimes more. As sales documents, they must be written in an upbeat marketing language, even if the author proposes a book that is serious, personal, and literary! To decode and demystify the book proposal's complexity, I wrote *Nonfiction Book Proposals Anybody Can Write*.

When a literary agent or editor at a publishing house responds positively to a query, the proposal is the next document that a writer sends. It contains:

- Concept Statement
- Proposal Table of Contents
- About the Book or Book Overview
- About the Author
- About the Market
- About the Competition
- About Promotion
- Production Details
- Table of Contents for the Book
- Chapter-by-Chapter Outline
- Sample Chapters
- Appendices

If you want to see your book published, understand that you are asking a publisher to assume the risk of financial failure as well as gain. Proposals, without the sample chapters, may be as long as twenty pages. Including the sample chapters, they take an average of about 120 hours to complete. For your investment of time and a small amount of resources, you can test publisher interest in your book idea, without having to write the book first. Yes, you must have sample chapters, usually three, but nonfiction writers, in contrast to novelists, can land a contract and an advance of money to finish their books with only a small sample of the actual book completed.

As in everything about writing and marketing, there is one exception: writers of memoir, autobiography, travel narratives, and creative nonfiction must often write half or even all of their books before a publisher will give them a contract. The reason for this is that the writing craft required to create an outstanding memoir is on a par with the demand to write a novel. A few sample chapters are no guarantee that a writer will be as skillful in subsequent chapters. Think about how well some explorers begin their journeys, with fanfare and kudos, then halfway along run into trouble.

In contrast, the sample chapters for how-to or information books are good indicators of how subsequent chapters will be written. Memoirs and creative nonfiction have much more art to their successful creation than how-to or information writing. Therefore, publishers wisely often request that more of the book be completed before they risk their pocketbooks.

When you have finished writing and revising your proposal, and have had it critiqued or professionally edited, and then have polished it, what's the next step? Never mail your proposal unless it has been specifically requested. In other words, if you've made a verbal pitch of your book at a conference and an agent asks you to send your proposal, then it has been solicited, and you can send it with a cover letter. However, if you have not talked with an editor or agent, you must query first. Send the proposal only when you receive a request to do so. Remember, include SASEs with any correspondence.

Results

Attitude, research, sales, and results. This last step of systematic marketing can be all important for keeping an accurate perspective on what you are doing. Your results should determine your next steps. In the early stages of marketing, you may have no trouble keeping track of your results. However, as you send more queries and have multiple manuscripts in the mail at once, you'd have to have a photographic memory to keep track of it all. Instead, keep records. Just set up a computer folder or file and keep notes.

What should go into such a file? The journalistic five Ws plus "how" will insure that you note basic information:

Who: Names of editors and agents, but also any descriptions of them, their companies, and what they seek. *Publishers Weekly* notes the comings and goings of editors and sometimes agents. Mastheads of magazines show current managing editors and department editors.

What: List what project you sent, its working title, sidebars, photos, which clips, and any other supplemental material that you sent. If you are marketing to magazines or newspapers, you could also build a file of specifications they seek, copying items from market guides, writer's guidelines, and directories.

Where: Addresses. Phone, fax, and cell numbers. E-mail and web addresses.

When: Note dates—when you mail queries, proposals, or manuscripts, when you receive correspondence, and future dates for follow-ups.

Why: You could use this heading to talk to yourself about your marketing strategy. On a day when you are clearheaded, you could write down why you chose the order of querying that you did. Why these publications in this order? Why these agents over others in *Guide to Literary Agents*?

How: How're you doing? You can use "how" to note anything else that doesn't fit in the above categories. If the last two items, "why" and "how," don't click for you, consider substituting "misc." for miscellaneous. It's good to include a catchall section.

I've found that writers often flounder when it comes to responding to letters and phone calls they receive. Even an acceptance can send a writer into a quandary. You may be asked to make a few changes. Unless they violate your principles or vision, do them. You may be asked to submit sources, check facts, or offer permission releases (for using copyrighted material or for the use of someone's photo). Fulfill this request as soon as possible.

When an editor or an agent phones or writes with an acceptance, it may come accompanied with an offer of terms and conditions. If these do not come in the form of a written contract, ask for one. Read it carefully, and seek advice on anything that you do not understand from published friends or from books on publishing, marketing, contracts, and rights. Even if you think you understand everything, double-check your knowledge. Be your own advocate. Consider joining the National Writers Union and using their member service of contract advisors, especially if you are seeking book publication.

Few are the writers who never have to deal with rejection letters. Most rejection letters are forms that tell you nothing helpful. They are a necessity to meet the reality of editors and agents receiving not thousands of queries and manuscripts a year but tens of thousands. The best response you can give to a form rejection is to allow yourself a few moments of disappointment, and then mail to the next publication or person on your list.

If you get nothing but form rejections and reach whatever number you deem as your reevaluation point (a dozen to several dozen, generally), you do need to consider what's going on. Are you marketing at the right level or to the right publications or people? If you've been aiming for the top, perhaps you should try the middle. If you've been querying nationally circulated magazines, perhaps it's time to look for regional magazines. If you've been striking out with literary agents, perhaps you should try querying editors at midsized and small publishing firms.

Form rejections may also signal a weak query letter. Scrap your old one and write a new one with more pizzazz. Consider the possibility that your idea—for an article or a book—is not yet refined enough. Reexamine your subject, your slant, and the scope and look for ways to improve your idea. Query letters and proposals, like the manuscripts themselves, put your writing on display. Too many form rejection letters nearly always suggest writing that is not strong enough—in originality, command of language, or knowledge of craft—to publish. Sometimes, the best decision you can make is to shelve a piece of writing, take more classes, develop new manuscripts, and try again. As I learned in a support group once, "Try fail. Try fail. Try succeed."

A different kind of rejection letter is the personalized rejection letter. An editor or agent has taken the time and gone to the trouble to give you feedback. Although you can claim your moment of disappointment in the rejection, any personal note is cause for hope if not celebration. In ninety-nine out of a hundred cases, a personal note means that the editor or agent found promise in your idea, your manuscript, or your writing. You're on the right track. If you are one to look for signs, this is one. Give serious consideration to the feedback, make changes, and resubmit if the person hasn't said not to. Make a note in your tracking file and send a new query or, if sought, a new manuscript to this editor or agent. You're building a relationship.

Acceptance, form rejections, or personalized rejections; at the end of the day, they are all part of a larger picture that is your career as a writer. In the next section, West, you'll have a chance to regain that perspective.

Marketing may or may not be a part of the writer's life that you enjoy. If your intention is to share your work or build a career as a writer, then marketing is certainly an unavoidable task. I believe that you can make it less odious and even enjoyable by increasing your skill at it. Incorporate marketing into your routine as a writer, allocating a certain amount of time to pursuing it. Make it systematic and you will succeed, and success at doing anything is its own reward.

MAP 13-1

Query for a How-To Article

This query was written by Dean Walker to the editor of Sesame Street Magazine's Parent's Guide *and resulted in a request to see the article, on speculation, and then acceptance and publication.*

Dear Ms. O'Connell:

My children, ages two and five, continually whack each other, either in anger or to get something they want. They're normal. I know because I work with children as a child development specialist in an elementary school. Even through the first grade, the kids, boys especially, are typically so aggressive in their interactions that a fourth-grade boy, who had the opportunity to observe a recess of 120 first graders later commented, "They're crazy out there!"

Interesting how children progress to the point where they view aggressive interactions as "crazy." How does it happen? Is it just a matter of growing up a little, or do parents need to take special measures to curb their children's hitting and shoving, pushing and poking? The article I would like to write for your readers asks just that question, and answers it with the help of researchers and mental-health therapists who specialize in aggression and children's development.

It's an important question, one that most parents of robust children must ask themselves at least occasionally. And it's a fact of life that children who do not learn to rein in their aggressive tendencies as they age are more and more rejected and isolated from their peers on a path that can lead to delinquency.

Researchers John Coie, Ph.D., and Craig Hart, Ph.D., define the two types of aggression as "instrumental aggression" and "hostile aggression." In talking with parents, I use the term "gimme" aggression to describe the instrumental type because it is basically the use of force to get something you want. Hostile aggression I have dubbed "gotcha" aggression because it describes well the desire that fuels hostile aggression—to "get" someone who is thought to be an enemy. Both researchers give advice to parents on how to avoid either type of aggression from becoming a pattern that lasts beyond the ages of six or seven.

MAP 13-1

Continued

My article of 1,800 words, tentatively titled, "When Push Comes to Shove," would begin with my personal worries about my own children's aggression, heightened by an anecdote about a fourth grader who has been rejected by peers because of aggression. Barbara Wanores, a veteran teacher, will be quoted about her experience with children who have not curbed their aggression by the later elementary years. What if my own children end up in that boat? Will they grow out of their hitting and fighting? How can I help them? I will find out from experts that my children are normal, and that a combination of development, modeling, and limit setting will keep my children from getting stuck in either the "gimme" or the "gotcha" styles of aggression.

Dr. Stephanie Sarnoff, a psychologist who specializes in children with ADHD (attention deficit hyperactivity disorder) will offer advice to parents whose children are more aggressive than others because of biochemical imbalances.

I am enclosing a clip of an article of mine that you published. I have also been published in *Parenting* magazine. I look forward to hearing from you concerning "When Push Comes to Shove." Thank you for your time and attention.

Sincere regards,

Dean Walker

Analysis: This clear and well-written query accomplished its purpose—selling the article. At 1,800 words, Dean Walker is proposing a major article. He has covered all of the bases: his personal and professional interest in the subject; the problem that parents of young children (the readers) struggle with that his article addresses; the research foundation for the article's ideas and his "reader-friendly" translation of the terms; how he plans to develop the article including the experts he intends to interview; and his prior publication credits. Notice, too, how the query reveals his voice and style—warm, supportive, and easy to understand—and a good match for the style of the magazine. Although this letter is a bit long, it is a strong query.

MAP 13-2

The Rules of Marketing

1. Use quality paper, generally twenty-pound bond, and white or off-white. Avoid "colors." Avoid scents. This is a conservative industry, and you're writing business correspondence.

2. Order printed letterhead stationery or design and print your own—*if* you can create a professional-looking end product. Include your name, address, phone number, e-mail, and web address (if you have one). Do not add mottos or monikers such as "Writer Extraordinaire," or "Have Quill Will Write," or even "Freelance Writer." They scream amateur.

3. For your query and cover letters, use business-style formatting. This means to use block style, which uses a left-justified margin for everything from the date to your signature. After the date, leave four line spaces. Then type the editor or agent's name, company, and address. Always send your letter to a person by name and position. Double-space and begin your salutation, punctuating with a colon, such as: "Dear Ms. Smith:". Next, double-space again and begin your lead. Use single-spacing for text and double-spacing between paragraphs. In block style, you have no indenting.

4. Always enclose a tri-folded self-addressed stamped envelope with the correct postage (or International Reply Coupons attached) for the addressee's country.

5. Never send an e-mail query unless one of the marketing guides, or the agent or editor, has directly instructed you to do so. Follow all instructions and guidelines.

6. Your name will be mud if you send out a query or cover letter with errors of punctuation or grammar. Proofread, and then proofread again. Don't rely solely on a spell-check program. Get a word whiz to read and edit your letters. Let them rest for a day or two and read them a final time before you print and mail.

7. Before you submit a requested article, essay, or book proposal, check your facts. Keep a log of your sources. Make sure you give attribution to quotes or paraphrasing.

MAP 13-2

Continued

8. Never telephone an editor or agent out of the blue to pitch your idea or suggest lunch or meeting. Once you have an editorial or agent relationship, keep telephone calls brief, professional, and to the point.
9. Never send food, clothing, or gifts as part of your query "package."
10. Never pitch two or three or more ideas for articles or books in the same query, and never ask the editor to suggest your slant.
11. Keep your personal problems to yourself. This includes all of your anxieties and insecurities about your writing and marketing.
12. Meet your deadlines. If you must be late, communicate that fact as soon as you know it.
13. Avoid defending or arguing in response to an editor or agent critique or request for revisions. Listen, thank them for their suggestions. Consider their advice and if you agree, make the revisions as quickly as possible and resubmit.
14. Remember your manners; express appreciation and send hand-written thank-you notes where appropriate.

WEST

Refining Your Vision

FOURTEEN

Exploring New Horizons

It only takes a drop of water
to start a waterfall.
Erin Brockovich

EVERYTHING YOU WRITE is a journey of discovery that leads to an opportunity to know yourself better. In Western society, our tendency is to see anything for sale as a product with a consumer market. As covered in East, you may need to treat your writing as a product and cultivate marketing skills to advance your goals.

A mistake that our society promotes is seeing the point of sale as the end of the process. For any artist, including writers of non-fiction, a piece of self has gone into each work. It may become a product, but it began as spirit. Even if 100,000 copies of a book are published, one exactly like another, the words on the page carry the author's individuality and spirit. A copy of a book is not like a Tupperware container or a doorknob or a shoe, even though all of these can be mass-produced.

Only by looking back from whence we came can we look forward. The nature of creative expression is to alter the creator. You are different at the end of creating any piece of writing than you were at the beginning. Although a long project, any book is likely to have a larger, more profound, effect on the writer than an article or essay, sometimes a short piece can be life altering.

In the parlance of Joseph Campbell's Hero's Journey, after the hero (includes heroines!) reaches the goal, he or she is reluctant to return home. Victorious, having vanquished the foe and claimed the reward, the last thing a hero wants to do is think about trudging homeward. When we have finished writing our articles, essays, and books, and perhaps when we have finished marketing them as well, human nature leads us to ignore the accomplishment in favor of pursuing the next one.

In the Hero's Journey, there is yet another test, the Ultimate Test, in which the hero is challenged to determine if he has learned and grown. If not, you have a human tragedy. No growth equals no change, no difference made, and no meaning. Stagnation. Doomed to repeat the same psychological mistakes again in different circumstances.

Your Ultimate Test after finishing your work, no matter its length or purpose, is to intentionally put it into perspective with your life. How do you do this? Is there a map for this part of the process?

Looking Back

First, review your reasons for writing. The review process is like an anchor that prevents you from drifting out to sea. Out of all the things, people, events, and ideas in the universe, why did you select the one you did? Even if you were given an assignment, you made it your own when you began to write. What was its promise to your readers? What difference did you hope it would make in their lives? What meaning can you claim from having finished your writing?

For example, I used to write a column for a newsletter. The purpose of my column, broadly speaking, was to supply a little information, a little entertainment, and a little inspiration. In other words, I sought to meet several of the four basic purposes, but I typically emphasized one over all others. When I wrote one column, "The Ergonomic Writer," I promised the reader information about repetitive strain disorders and workplace equipment that could relieve it. The difference I hoped to achieve for my readers was relief from problems that could in the extreme render them physically unable to write.

The meaning I carried away from finishing this column was satisfaction on many levels. First, I completed my obligation. Looking deeper into this statement, my promise to write a monthly column means that I am a person who keeps my word. That has great meaning to me and is a source of personal pride.

I wrote about repetitive strain and ergonomic solutions because I had years of problems with shoulder, neck, and back pain for which I found at least partial relief when I changed my equipment. Although I made these changes before I wrote the column, further research filled out areas that I didn't know. As a result, I discovered a Kinesis keyboard I intend to get. Thus, writing about ergonomics increased my own knowledge and led to improvement of my working life. It also gave me a different kind of writer tip to post on my web site.

A powerful step to take when you have finished a piece of writing is to give yourself a pat on the back. Self-crediting completes the circle. Failure to give recognition to a finished work can represent self-sabotage and become a setup for worse problems dealing with yourself down the road. If you ignore completions—"it's nothing," you might say—you weaken your resolve to finish what you write. Granted, some of us have more problems finishing projects while others have greater problems beginning them. Perhaps both difficulties are connected through the acknowledgment of completion.

In my former critique groups, we popped a cork to celebrate the completion of a first draft of any book. It was an interesting study of human behavior to note who wanted to brush off this ritual. To finish a project as long as a book is a giant accomplishment. To finish an essay or poem or article may be as meaningful as finishing a book.

Several years ago, about a week after I'd had surgery, I wrote an essay about a former traumatic experience. One of my children had been in crisis, and the shock waves still rocked my psyche. The essay was my first attempt to express any of my experience, and the act was healing. I'd thought about the events and been urged to write about them for years. Eeking out and finishing this first essay was as giant an emotional accomplishment as if I had written a 500-page book.

Completion and acknowledging completion frees me emotionally to write about this topic again. If I had not given myself that pat on the back, I would have carried emotional baggage into the next round—if I ever allowed myself to return to the topic.

Not all writing projects are meant to be finished. Like visual artists, we writers may begin a piece and discard it, knowing that it wasn't working the way we envisioned it, or for other reasons. Perhaps another idea emerges out of the first and is the stronger of the two.

The act of looking back involves seeing a particular work in its place in the body of your writing. If you have just begun to write, that body of work may contain just a few items. It doesn't matter if you have a few finished pieces or many. It doesn't matter if you have three times as many unfinished pieces as completed ones. When you complete a work, take the long view of your writing to this point in time. Ask yourself some leading questions:

Do you see a pattern? Is the most recent piece similar to others in the past? Through it, are you exploring a particular theme, a specific type of writing, or fulfilling a purpose you set for yourself? Does this piece of writing define the beginning, the middle, or the end of a pattern? Is the recent work a departure from prior writing? If so, are you setting out in a new direction or is it a one-of-a-kind for now?

With these answers and an overview of your body of work, here come the hard questions. Why do you think you are writing in this pattern? Are you fulfilling a script that was written by one of your parents that is represented in this pattern, this body of work? What need are you supplying in your own life story? What yearning does writing this particular piece fulfill?

A friend of mine shared the story of her mother getting her palm read soon after she got married. The palm reader told her mother that one of her children would be famous. Since then, my friend's writing life has been colored by her mother's expectations.

Her mother repeatedly tells her, "I want you to publish before I die."

Perhaps your completed piece fits in your work world. Will this recent manuscript and the body of your work facilitate your career, your vocation? If so, is it satisfying—is it enough—to write for this reason? What writing, if any, did you put aside to fulfill your vocational goals? Does the most recent completion supply your goals? At what time will you return to the projects you put aside?

I've known a number of writers who began writing for work reasons, who acquired skills and proficiency, and discovered that they could now express deeper aspects of themselves. They were able to shift to writing essays, memoirs, or novels—for self-expression and recreation. One therapist I know began writing a self-help book, but it wasn't working out. Rather than finish it, she put the project aside. She gave herself permission to take a course in screenplay writing and had a blast. When she started another self-help book related to her therapeutic work, the writing exploded with vitality. She brought her creative success from the screenplay, along with fictional skills, into her nonfiction writing. I call this cross-pollination. The hybrid is almost always stronger.

Looking Forward

Once you finish looking back, developing perspective of your recent writing in terms of your past works, you have the best platform for looking forward. What goal will you set your sights on next? Now you can decide whether you want to develop something that will fit a pattern of writings from your past or whether you want to strike out in an entirely different direction.

Many writers get stuck at this next step. Decision-making can be difficult. What if you have half a dozen different ideas about what to write next? How do you decide? What if you draw a blank?

You can take one of three actions and each one produces a different outcome. (1) You can do nothing. (2) You can choose any project. (3) You can evaluate and then choose.

Doing nothing might mean that you don't want to choose what

to write, or it could mean that you'd rather do something other than writing. Perhaps you'd rather go sailing, so to speak. Perhaps some internal process of sorting is going on and it isn't time to choose. Perhaps other factors have put up roadblocks that prevent you from reaching a decision. Some people incorrectly call doing nothing "writer's block." A choice underlies not choosing and not writing. Self-examination will usually rout out what's really going on.

Second, you can make a choice while still not knowing which of many options is best. Spinning wheels, after all, only digs deeper holes. Let's say that you pick one of three different pieces of writing. You have no particular reason why you chose one over the others. The positive effect of jumping in is that you're being productive. You're writing; you're engaged in the process and developing your skills. The negative effect is that you have given no thought to your direction and the difference you wish to make. But you are keeping busy.

Third, you can evaluate your choices and then choose. Evaluating is hard work but worth it! By what criteria do you select one of three seemingly equal possibilities? If you have looked back at your body of work and your past choices, you have a wonderful perspective for evaluating a next step. You can continue existing patterns for preexisting reasons and can expect a similar result. For instance, the four-book Writer's Compass series stands alone as well as continues the pattern of writing accessible, detailed, and practical information that I began with my prior two books. All six, when I finish the Compass series, will therefore fit a same pattern. Yet, this book on writing nonfiction is the first of the new pattern of four books because it begins a series. Why did I propose this new pattern? My first two books addressed marketing, and I wanted to write about how to write and how to revise. Once I finish these four, will I continue in this same pattern, or will I choose a different type of writing? I'll make that choice when I regain perspective after I complete book four.

Another way to select a next project is to ask what the downstream effect would be of writing one thing over another. For instance, at any given time, I could spew out a list of half a dozen projects (or more, God help me) that tickle my fancy. Looking downstream in terms of time alone helps me put them in order of development.

I find that my most helpful analysis is to determine what the difference will be if I choose one project over another. Once again, instead of asking *how* I can do something or even *why*, the new-paradigm question about *differences* produces an answer about meaning. I certainly want to make choices that are meaningful in ways that fit my values and direction.

If you have not already signed a contract or accepted an assignment, you have great latitude, but you do not have unlimited time and energy. These are too precious to squander. Everybody has a different value system, but to not consider your next steps in terms of your value system is a mistake. What project would fulfill your values best?

For instance, many writers with aging parents decide that they better get their elders' stories soon or lose the chance forever. Some writers reach the same decision about their own lives and decide it's time to write a memoir or autobiography. They value the legacy of their life experiences and that of their family members enough to make a choice to do this writing over some other writing.

When you make a choice and think that you can settle into the process of researching and writing, expect several contradictory things to happen. First, you are likely to have your decision tested. During lunch with a friend, you'll mention your choice, and the friend will be less than enthusiastic. Did you really make the right decision? Or, the phone will ring and the organization you volunteer for will ask if you can take over the newsletter—just for one month, mind you.

Joseph Campbell calls these tests of your commitment "threshold guardians." It's as if you are being asked, "Are you sure?" That's a valuable question. My threshold guardians take the form of sirens suggesting that I go on vacation. Call them escape fantasies for a restless soul or the need for rest and revitalizing for an overworked person.

With your new writing project decided, you're at the beginning of a next journey, but you are not the same person as began the last journey. You have more skill and greater understanding of your self, your subject, and perhaps of life itself. In many cultures, no journey is begun without a send-off. It may be the *puja* blessing in India, ceremonial bowing, or a send-off spaghetti dinner! My son asked me once why I always vacuum and wash my car before I go on a road trip when I'm just going to get the car dirty. It's the way I honor beginnings.

Another thing that happens after you have committed to a next piece of writing is serendipity. Unexpected and fortuitous events pop up and give you the very confirmation of your writing that the threshold guardians would deny you. One of my friends was working on a novel about a woman who was a zealous doctor's first cryogenic experiment. On an airplane flight, she chatted with the man seated next to her only to learn that he was an executive in a company that specialized in cryogenics.

You might believe in coincidence; I believe in serendipity and see it as a feature of the process and a welcome gift. Expect the unexpected. Make room for it and your writing will go easier for it.

I leave you with these well-known but powerful thoughts by Goethe who, by the way, wrote *Faust* in his eighties:

> Until one is committed
> there is hesitancy, the chance to draw back
> always ineffectiveness.
> Concerning all acts of initiative (and creation),
> there is one elementary truth,
> the ignorance of which kills countless ideas
> and splendid plans:
> that the moment one definitely commits oneself,
> then Providence moves too.
> All sorts of things occur to help one
> that would never otherwise have occurred.
> A whole stream of events issue from the decision,
> raising in one's favor all manner
> of unforeseen incidents and meetings
> and material assistance,

which no man could have dreamt
would have come his way.
Whatever you can do, or dream you can do, begin it.
Boldness has genius, power, and magic in it.

Beginnings of journeys are exciting—and sometimes nerve-wracking. Endings are satisfying, but may also leave us sad because they are over, and the new adventure is not yet known. Celebrate the process: brainstorming, selecting an idea and a slant, researching, outlining. Give your all to your writing and trust that in revision, you'll find the gem and polish it. When you've finished marketing and done everything you envisioned, take a moment to appreciate the wonder of it all—your writing, your life, and you, the creator of your words who had the courage to go the distance, and will again.

INDEX

Page numbers in *italic* indicate maps; those in **bold** indicate tables.

ABOUT THE AUTHOR

As an independent book editor, Elizabeth Lyon serves writers in the United States and abroad through her company, Editing International, LLC, www.4-edit.com. Scores of writers credit her help with their success in getting published, winning contests, and securing movie options.

Lyon's first book for writers, *Nonfiction Book Proposals Anybody Can Write,* is considered the standard reference on preparing proposals. Literary agent Jean Naggar describes her second book, *The Sell Your Novel Tool Kit,* as an indispensable guide that belongs on every writer's bookshelf.

As an instructor and keynote speaker, Elizabeth Lyon is known for her clear, practical instruction, inspirational encouragement, and good humor. A contributor to *Writer's Digest* magazine and *The Writer,* Lyon also writes columns, essays, and articles for newsletters and online e-zines. In addition, readers may find helpful tips posted at her author web site: www.elizabethlyon.com.

Born in Toledo, Ohio, she lives in Eugene, Oregon, with her beloved Border collie.